Contents

Unit: Needs of Living Things	2	WI...	
Unit: Energy	27	STEM Occupation Riddle Cards	
Unit: Materials, Objects, and Structures	52	A Web Organizer About...	111
Unit: Daily and Seasonal Changes	76	STEM Vocabulary	112
		How Am I Doing?	113
Engineering in Our Daily Lives	96	STEM Rubric	114
Think Like an Engineer!	97	STEM Focus	115
The Design Process	98	Achievement Awards	116
Engineering Challenges	102		
Promoting STEM Occupations	103	Answer Key	117
STEM-Related Occupations	104		

Teacher Tips

Encourage Topic Interest

Help students develop an understanding and appreciation of different STEM concepts by providing an area in the classroom to display topic-related non-fiction books, pictures, collections, and artifacts as a springboard for learning.

What I Think I Know / What I Would Like to Know Activity

Introduce each STEM unit by asking students what they think they know about the topic, and what they would like to know about the topic. Complete this activity as a whole-group brainstorming session, in cooperative small groups, or independently. Once students have had a chance to complete the questions, combine the information to create a class chart for display. Throughout the study, periodically update students' progress in accomplishing their goal of what they want to know, and validate what they think they know.

Vocabulary List

Keep track of new and theme-related vocabulary on chart paper for students' reference. Encourage students to add theme-related words. Classify the word list into the categories of nouns, verbs, and adjectives. In addition, have students create their own STEM dictionaries as part of their learning logs.

Learning Logs

Keeping a learning log is an effective way for students to organize thoughts and ideas about the STEM concepts presented and examined. Students' learning logs also provide insight on what follow-up activities are needed to review and to clarify concepts learned.

Learning logs can include the following types of entries:

- Teacher prompts
- Students' personal reflections
- Questions that arise
- Connections discovered
- Labelled diagrams and pictures
- Definitions for new vocabulary

© Chalkboard Publishing

Living Things

All living things need air, water, and food.
All living things grow and change.

| People are living things. | Animals are living things. | Plants are living things. |

Think About It!

1. What do all living things need?

_____

2. Is a squirrel a living thing? How do you know?

_____

_____

_____

"Living Things"—Think About It! (continued)

3. Look at the pictures below. Circle the things that are living. Tell a partner how you know each thing is alive.

a) toy car

b) teddy bear

c) man

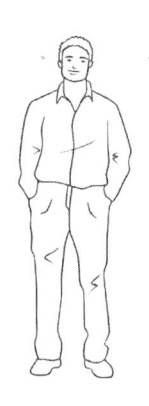

d) dog

e) feather

f) stool

g) cow

h) flower

© Chalkboard Publishing

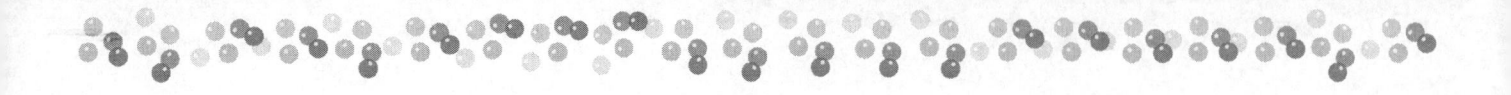

Living Things Collage

Look for pictures of living things in magazines. Cut out the pictures and paste them below.

Write a sentence about living things.

_____

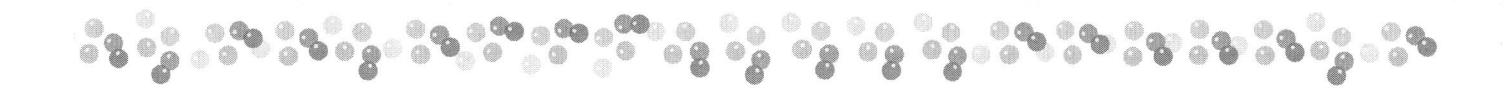

Non-living Things Collage

Look for pictures of non-living things in magazines. Cut out the pictures and paste them below.

Write a sentence about non-living things.

_____

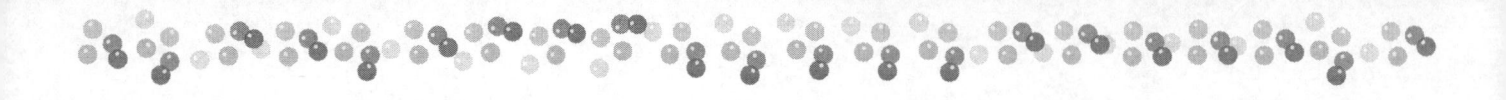

My Body

Draw a line from each label to the right part of the body.

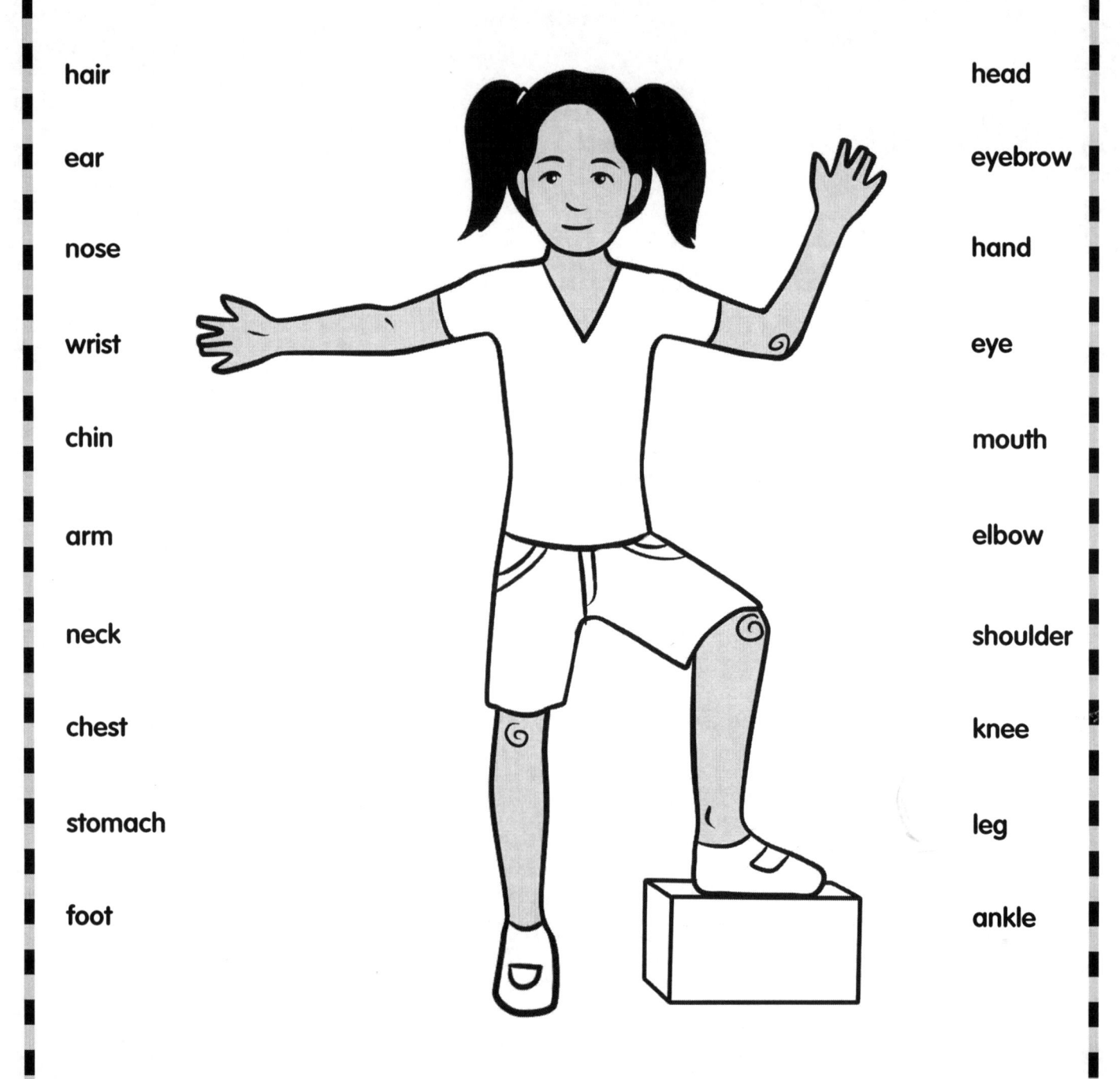

hair

ear

nose

wrist

chin

arm

neck

chest

stomach

foot

head

eyebrow

hand

eye

mouth

elbow

shoulder

knee

leg

ankle

Your Body Helps You

Your brain helps you to learn and think.

Your lungs help you breathe.

Your heart pumps blood around your body.

Your muscles help your body move.

Your stomach and intestines digest the food you eat.

Your bones help hold up your body.

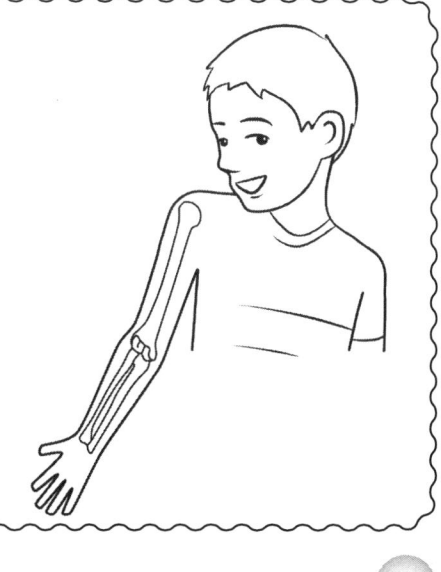

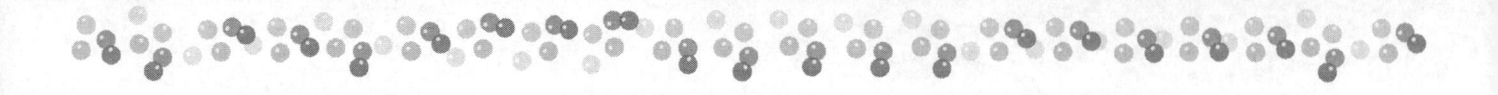

"Your Body Helps You"—Think About It!

Solve each riddle. Use the words below.

bones   fingers   brain   muscles   lungs   heart   teeth

1. We help your body move. _____

2. You use us to bite an apple. _____

3. I help you to learn and think. _____

4. I help you hold a brush. _____

5. We help you breathe. _____

6. I help you pump blood around your body. _____

7. We help hold up your body. _____

Brain Stretch

Arms help you to reach and to carry things. Feet help you to stand and move so you do not fall.

Tell a partner what ways other body parts help you.

Your Five Senses

Cut out and paste pictures from magazines to show each of the senses.

Sight

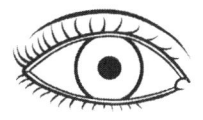

I use my eyes to see things.

Here are some things I can see.

Hearing

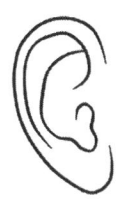

I use my ears to hear things.

Here are some things I can hear.

Touch

I use my fingers to touch things.

Here are some things I can touch.

continued next page

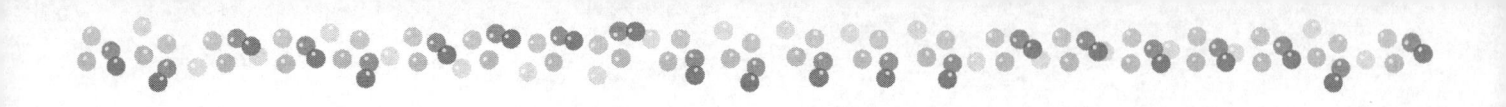

Smell

I use my nose to smell things.
Here are some things I can smell.

Taste

I use my tongue to taste things.
Here are some things I can taste.

Think About It!

1. I see with my _____.

2. I hear with my _____.

3. I touch with my _____.

4. I smell with my _____.

5. I taste with my _____.

continued next page

"Your Five Senses"—Think About It! (continued)

6. Choose the sense that goes with each pair of pictures. Use each sense only once. Use the words below.

hearing   sight   smell   taste   touch

a) _____

b) _____

c) _____

d) _____

e) _____

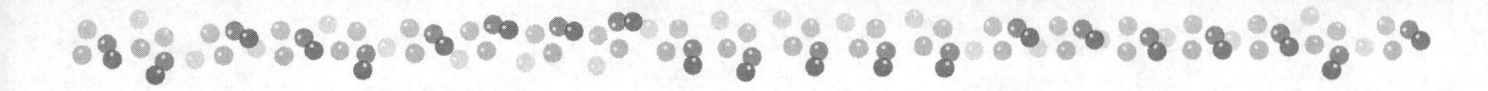

Listen for Sounds

What do sounds tell us?

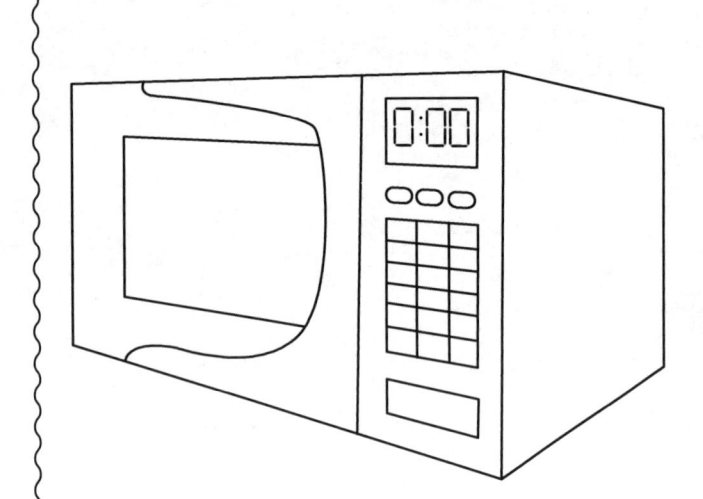

Beep!
The food is hot.

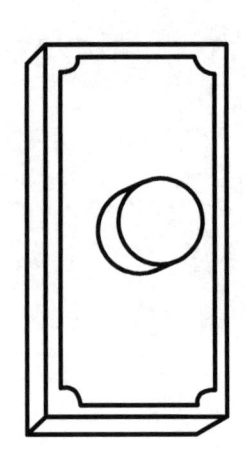

Ding dong!
Someone is at the door.

Ring! Ring!
Someone is calling.

Beep! Beep! Beep!
It is time to get up.

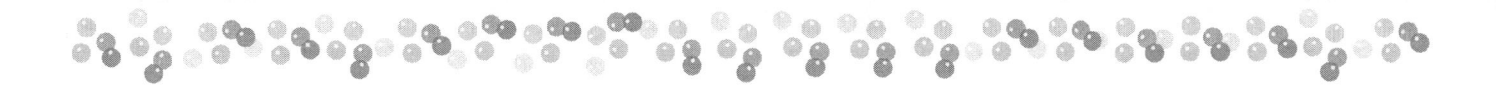

"Listen for Sounds"—Think About It!

Use the words to complete the sentences.

fire   car   cross   start

1. I hear a **siren**.

   A police _____ is coming.

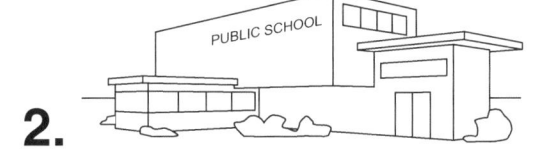

2. I hear a **school bell**.

   It is time for school to _____.

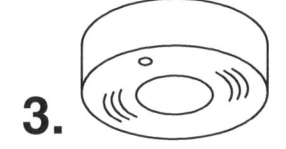

3. I hear a **smoke detector**.

   There is a _____.

4. I hear a **whistle**.

   Cars must stop to let children _____.

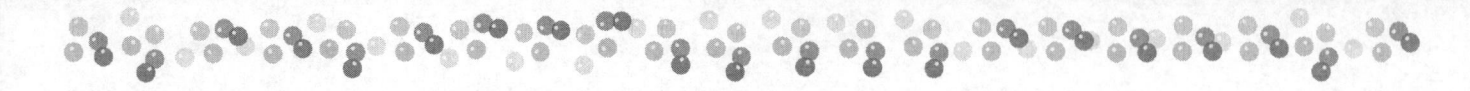

Animals On the Move

All animals have body parts to help them. Animals move in different ways.

Fish have fins to help them swim.

Birds have wings to help them fly.

Snakes use their body to slither.

Many animals walk on legs.

1. Draw a line to match the animal to the way it can move.

   a) This animal can hop.

   b) This animal moves slowly.

   c) This animal can move fast.

   d) This animal can climb.

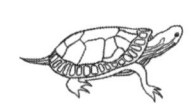

Compare Living Things

Compare two living things. For example,

- Compare two animals.
- Compare two plants.
- Compare an animal to a human.

Comparing		
What is the size of it?		
What does it look like?		
How are they the same?		
How are they different?		

Parts of a Plant

The picture shows four main parts of a flowering plant.

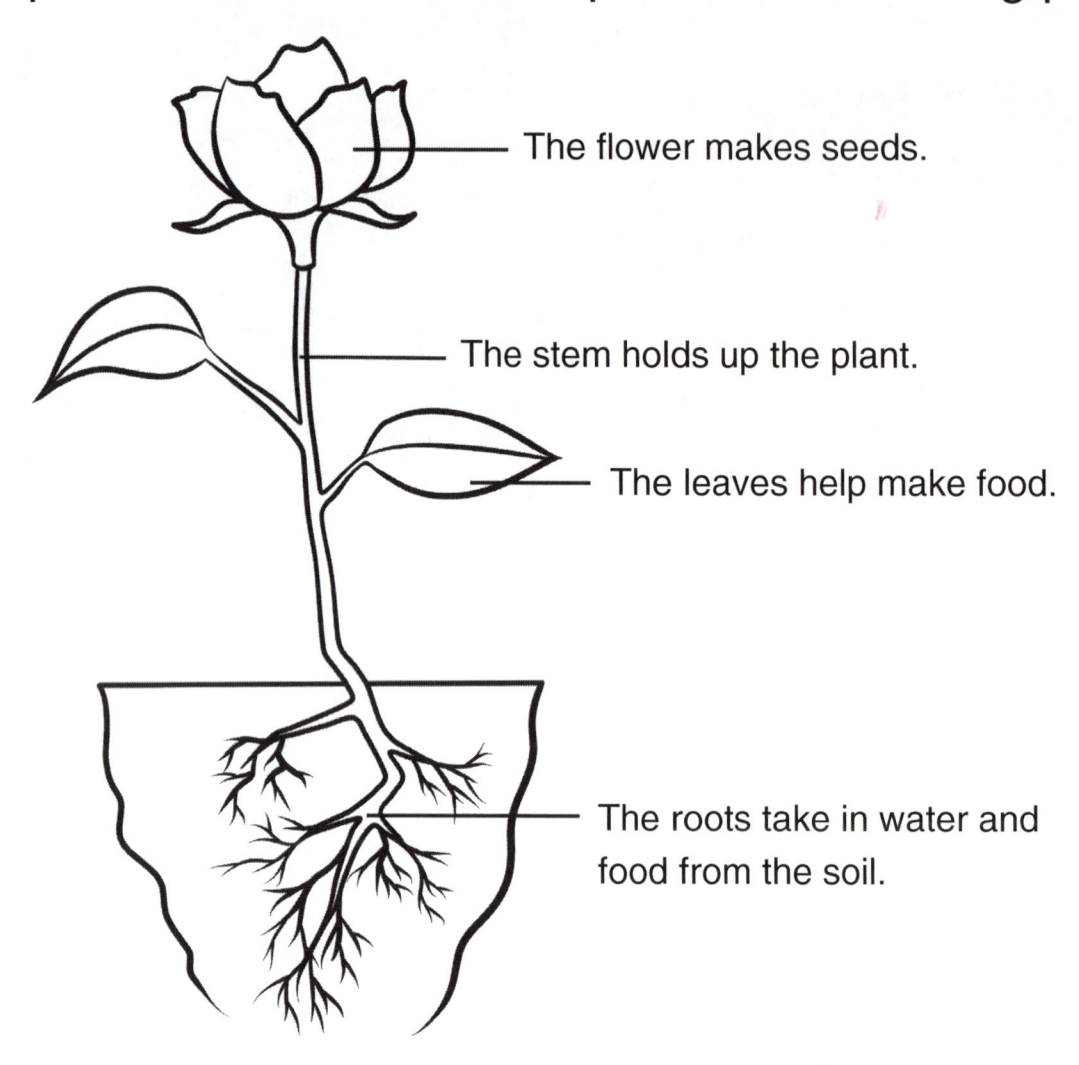

The flower makes seeds.

The stem holds up the plant.

The leaves help make food.

The roots take in water and food from the soil.

Did You Know?

Bright flowers attract bees.
Bees help plants make seeds.

"Parts of a Plant"—Think About It!

1. Label the plant. Use the words below.

flower   leaves   roots   stem

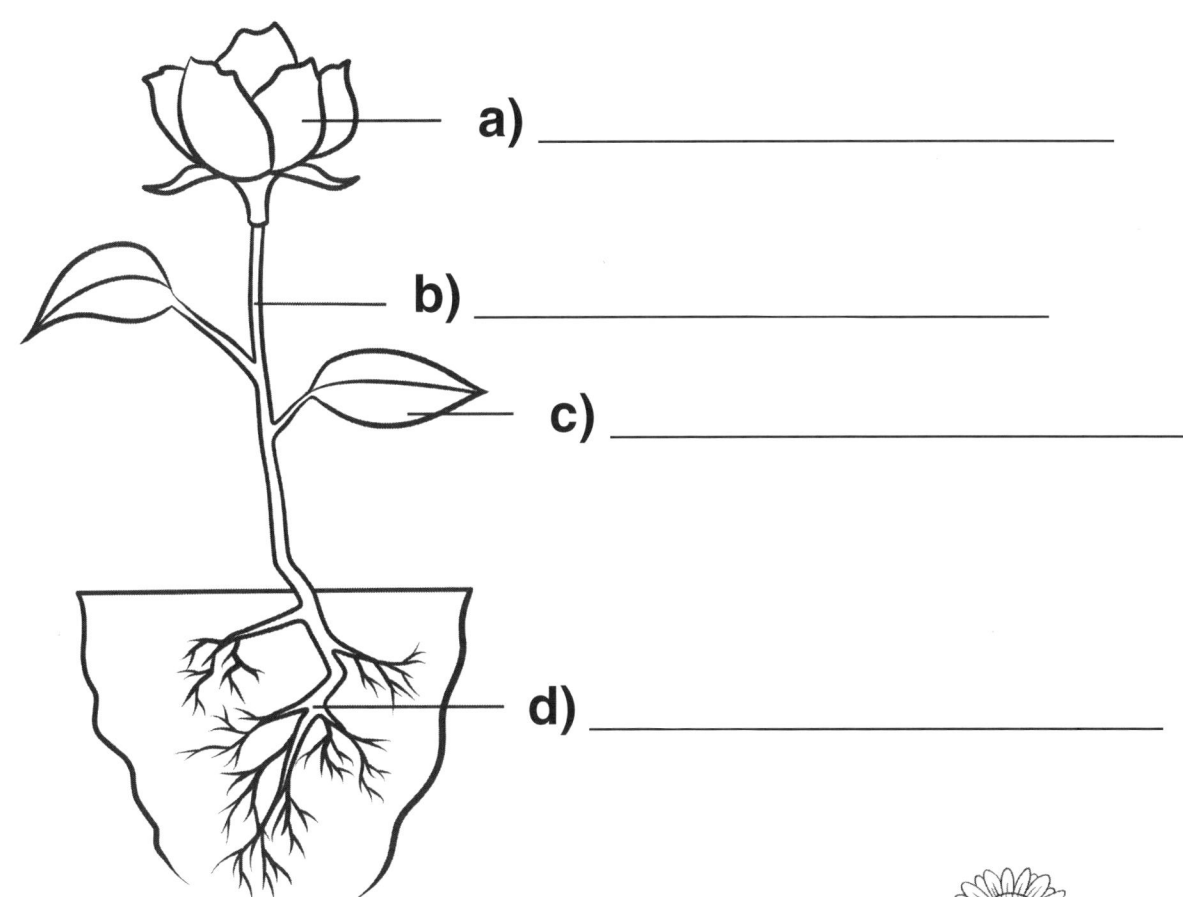

a) _____

b) _____

c) _____

d) _____

2. Plants can be different from each other.

Compare these two plants.

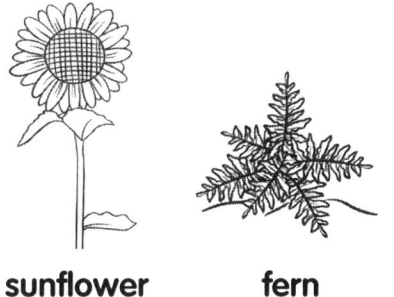

sunflower   fern

One way they are the same: _____

One way they are different: _____

Experiment: How Do Plants Take Up Water?

The stem holds up the plant.
Find out what other ways the stem helps the plant.

What You Need

- Celery stalk
- Clear glass
- Water
- Red food colouring

What You Do

1. Put water in a glass.
2. Add ten drops of red food colouring.
3. Put the celery stalk in the water.
4. Use the stalk to stir the water.
5. Wait two hours. Ask an adult to cut a bit off the end of the stalk. Tell what you see.

_____

_____

6. Wait four hours. Repeat step 3. Tell what you see.

_____

_____

7. Wait until the next day. Look at the celery.

"Experiment: How Do Plants Take Up Water?"—Think About It!

1. Draw what you saw happen the next day. Colour your picture.

2. What does this tell you?
What does the stem do to help the plant?

_____

_____

What Happened?

- Tiny tubes in the stem carry the water up the stalk.
- Each tube works like a drinking straw.

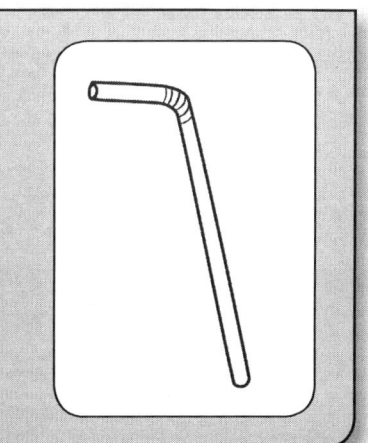

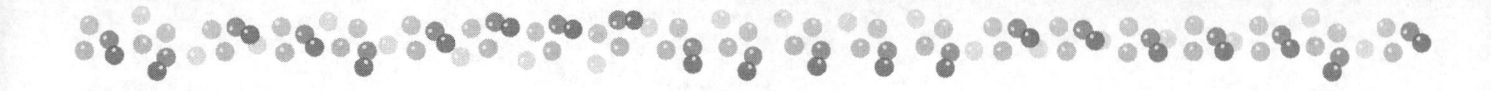

Needs of Living Things

Living things need air, food, and water.
Living things need a place to live.
Living things also need space to grow.

Animals and plants find what they need in their environment. This is the area where they live.

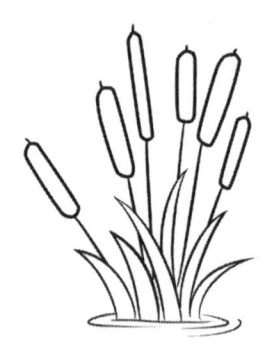

A pond is a home for cattails.

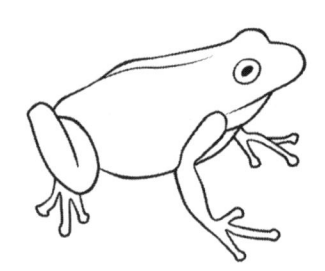

A pond is a home for frogs.

Brain Stretch

How does a chipmunk get what it needs to live?
(**Hint:** It needs food, air, water, and shelter.)

_____

_____

_____

chipmunk

Animals Live in Different Places

1. Draw a line from the animal to where it lives.

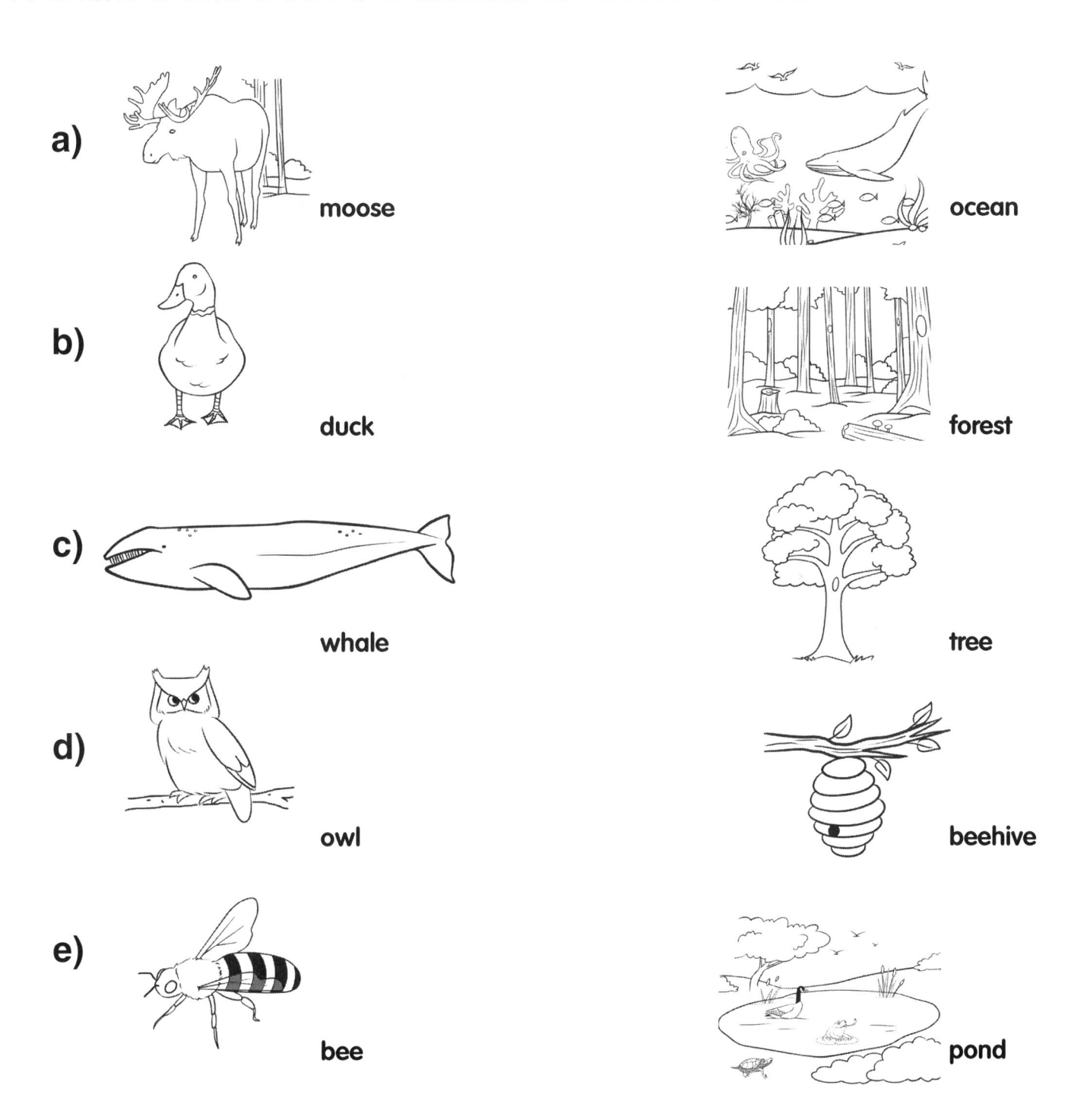

a) moose

b) duck

c) whale

d) owl

e) bee

ocean

forest

tree

beehive

pond

© Chalkboard Publishing

A Healthy Environment

Animals and plants need a healthy environment.

What Animals Most Need	What Plants Most Need
• clean air • clean water • safe food to eat • shelter • space to grow	• clean air • clean water • sunlight to help make food • food in the soil to grow • space to grow

Think About It!

1. Draw and colour an animal. Show where it lives. Label all the things it needs to live.

People Can Harm Living Things

Do	Do Not
• Put garbage in a trash can 	• Put garbage in the water that living things drink and live in 
• Walk on hiking trails in a park and look at wildflowers 	• Walk on plants or pick wildflowers 

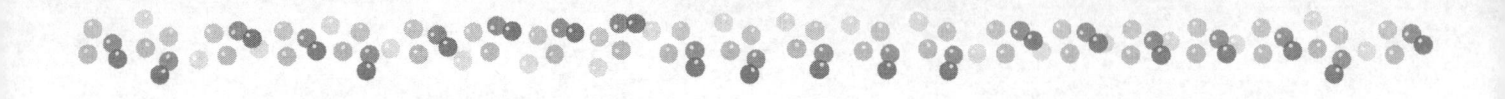

"People Can Harm Living Things"—Think About It!

1. This picture shows polluted water. How might the pollution harm the fish that live in that water?

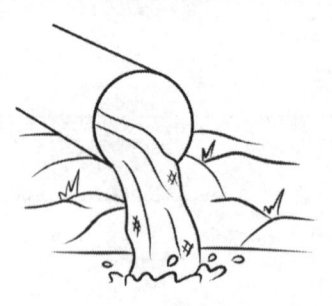

_____

2. Draw a way to help the environment.

3. Write a sentence that tells about your picture.

_____

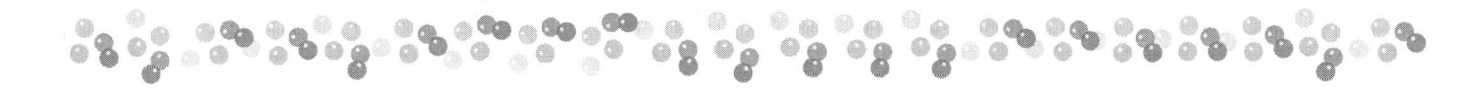

Taking Care of Living Things

1. Draw a picture to show how to take care of a pet.

I take care of a pet by

_____.

2. Draw a picture to show how to take care of a plant.

I take care of a plant by

_____.

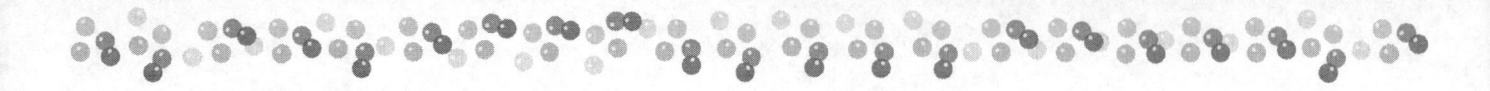

What I Learned About Living Things

1. Fill in the blanks. Use the words below.

   air   environment   plants   stem   water

   a) Animals and _____ are living things.

   b) All living things need _____ and _____.

   c) The _____ of a plant brings water up the plant.

   d) Living things get what they need from their

   _____.

2. Draw the body part you use for each sense below.

   a) I smell a pizza.

   b) I look at the stars.

   c) I listen to a bird sing.

What Is Energy?

Energy makes things happen.

Energy makes us move.
Energy makes things work.

You need energy to run.

A video game needs energy to work.

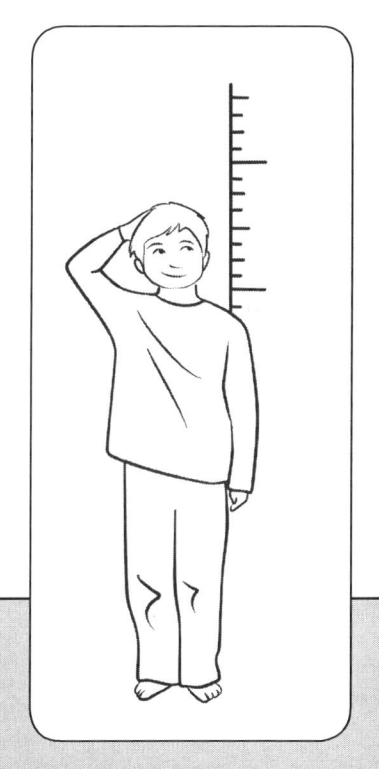

Energy makes all living things grow.

Brain Stretch

How do you get the energy you need to grow?

_____

_____

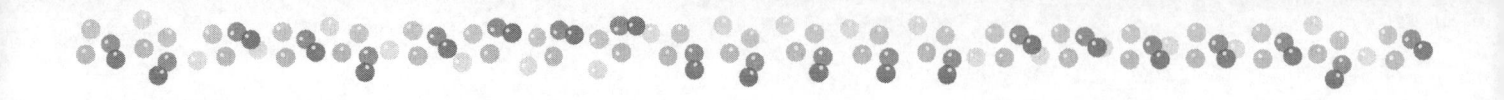

"What Is Energy?"—Think About It!

Complete each sentence. Use the words below.

energy   jump   create

1. You need energy to _____.

2. A plant needs _____ to grow.

3. A light bulb needs energy to _____ light.

4. Look at the pictures below.
   Circle the activities that use a lot of energy.

A.

B.

C.

D.

E.

F.

Where Energy Comes From

Energy comes from different sources.
A source is the place where something comes from.

Sun	gasoline	electricity
wind	battery	food

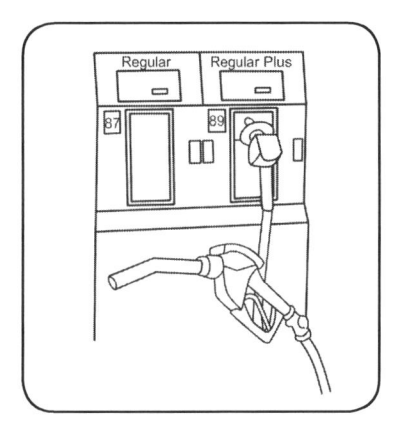

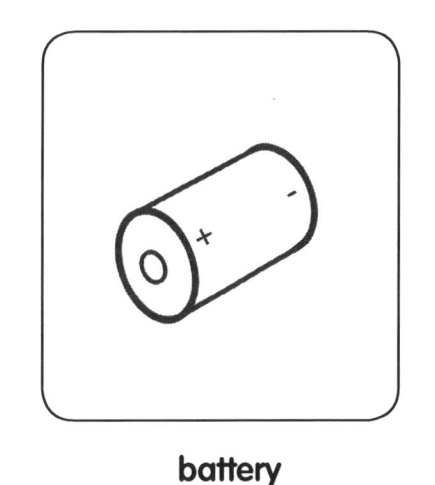

Think About It!

1. Colour each source of energy you use.
2. Tell a partner how you use each energy source.

We Get Energy from the Sun

The Sun is the main source of energy for all living things.

The Sun warms the air.
The Sun warms the land and water.

The Sun gives us light.
The Sun makes it possible to grow food.

Think About It!

1. Draw pictures to show three things that the Sun does.

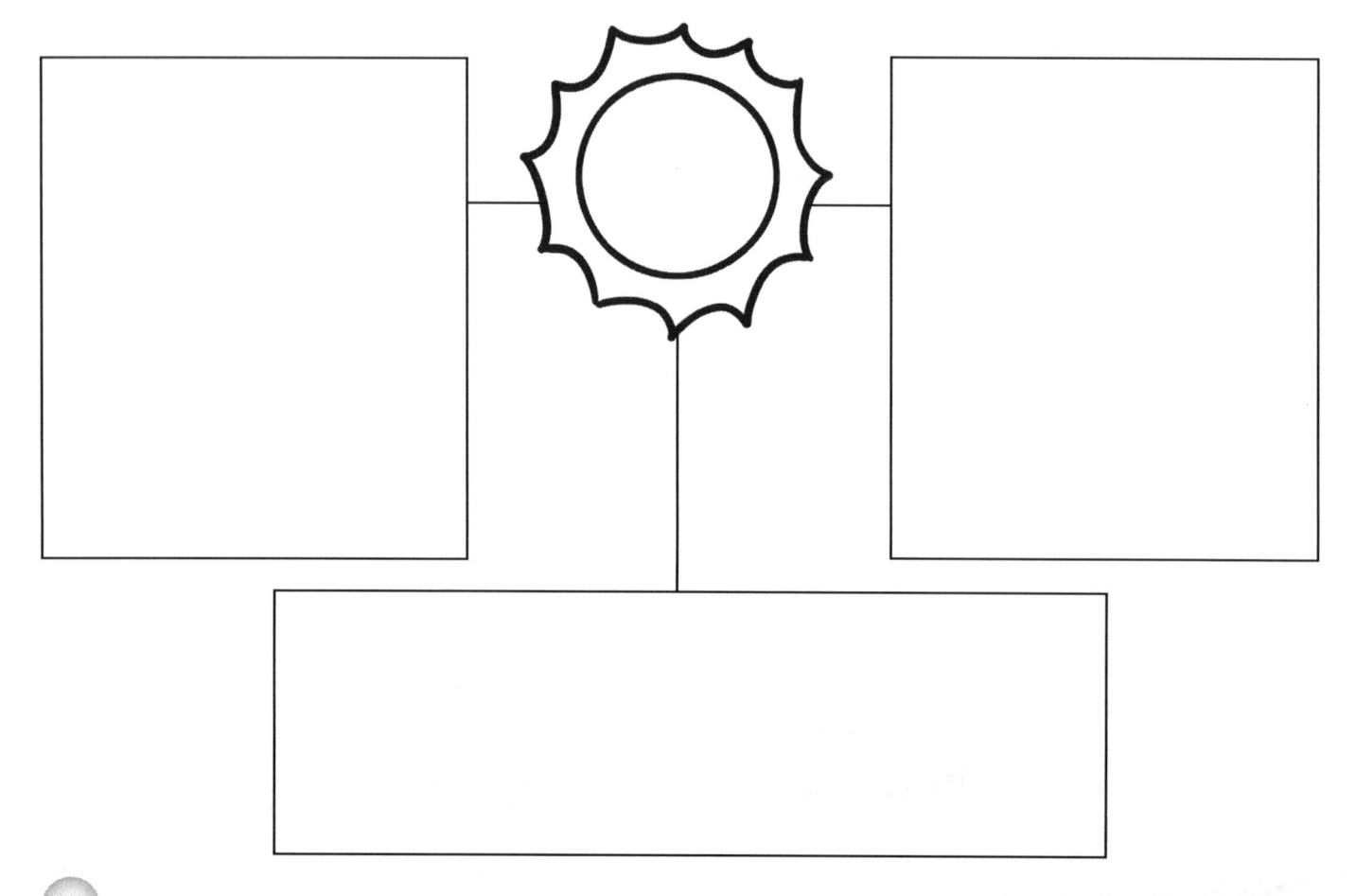

Experiment: What Does Sunlight Do to Water?

Find out what sunlight does to water.

What You Need

- 2 plastic cups containing equal amounts of water
- Thermometer

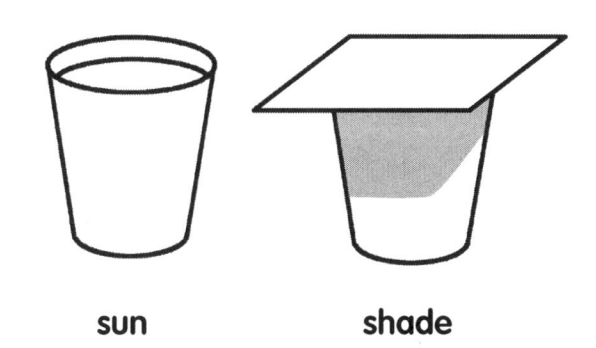

sun   shade

What You Do

1. Ask an adult to help you take the temperature of the water in both cups. The temperature should be the same in both cups.//
2. Put one cup of water in a sunny spot.
3. Put the other cup of water in a shady spot.
4. Predict what will happen to the temperature of the water in each cup.
5. Wait two hours. Then take the temperature of the water again.

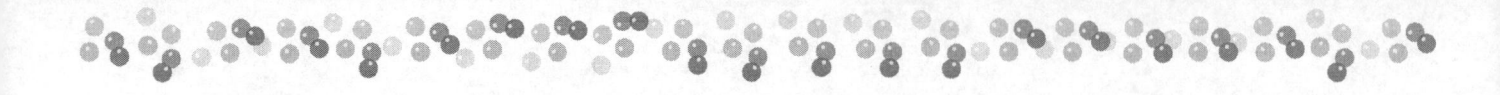

"Experiment: What Does Sunlight Do to Water?"—Think About It!

1. What do you predict will happen?

_____

2. Use the chart below to record the results.

Starting Temperature		Temperature After Two Hours	
Sunlight	Shade	Sunlight	Shade

3. What do the results tell you about sunlight?

_____

4. Use the words below to fill in the blanks.

cool   **warm**

a) I get _____   b) I stay _____

when I am in the sunlight.   when I am in the shade.

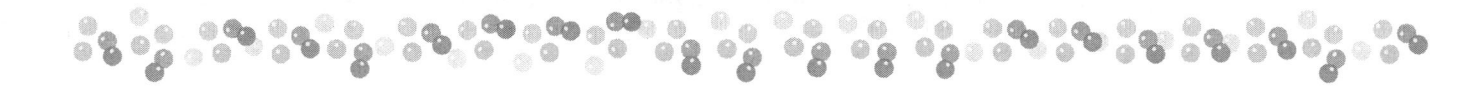

Experiment: What Does Sunlight Do to Plants?

The Sun gives us light.
Find out what sunlight does to plants.

What You Need

- 2 plants
- Water

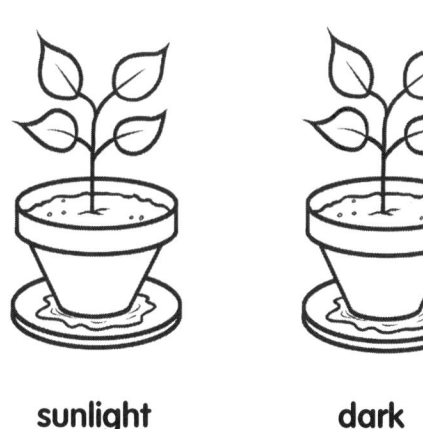

sunlight   dark

What You Do

1. Put one plant close to a window.
   This plant will get sunlight.

2. Put the other plant in the dark.

3. Water each plant once a week.

4. Predict what will happen to the plants.

5. Compare the plants each week.

6. Do this for three weeks.

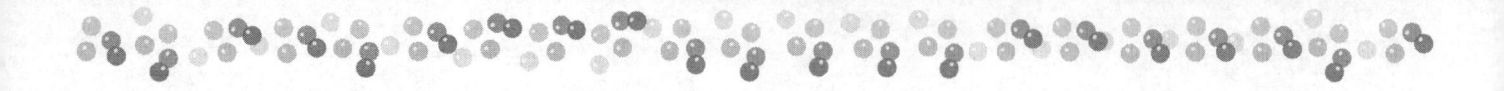

"Experiment: What Does Sunlight Do to Plants?"—Think About It!

1. What do you predict will happen?

_____

2. Draw a picture of each plant after three weeks.

Sunlight	Dark

3. Compare the pictures.
What happened to the plant that did not get sunlight?

_____

_____

4. What did you learn? Fill in the blank.

Plants need _____ to live and grow.

We Get Energy from Food

We need energy to do things.
We use energy to walk.
We even use energy to sleep.

All living things need energy to grow.
We get energy from food.

Look at the picture below.
The picture shows an energy chain.
Trace the flow of energy from the Sun.

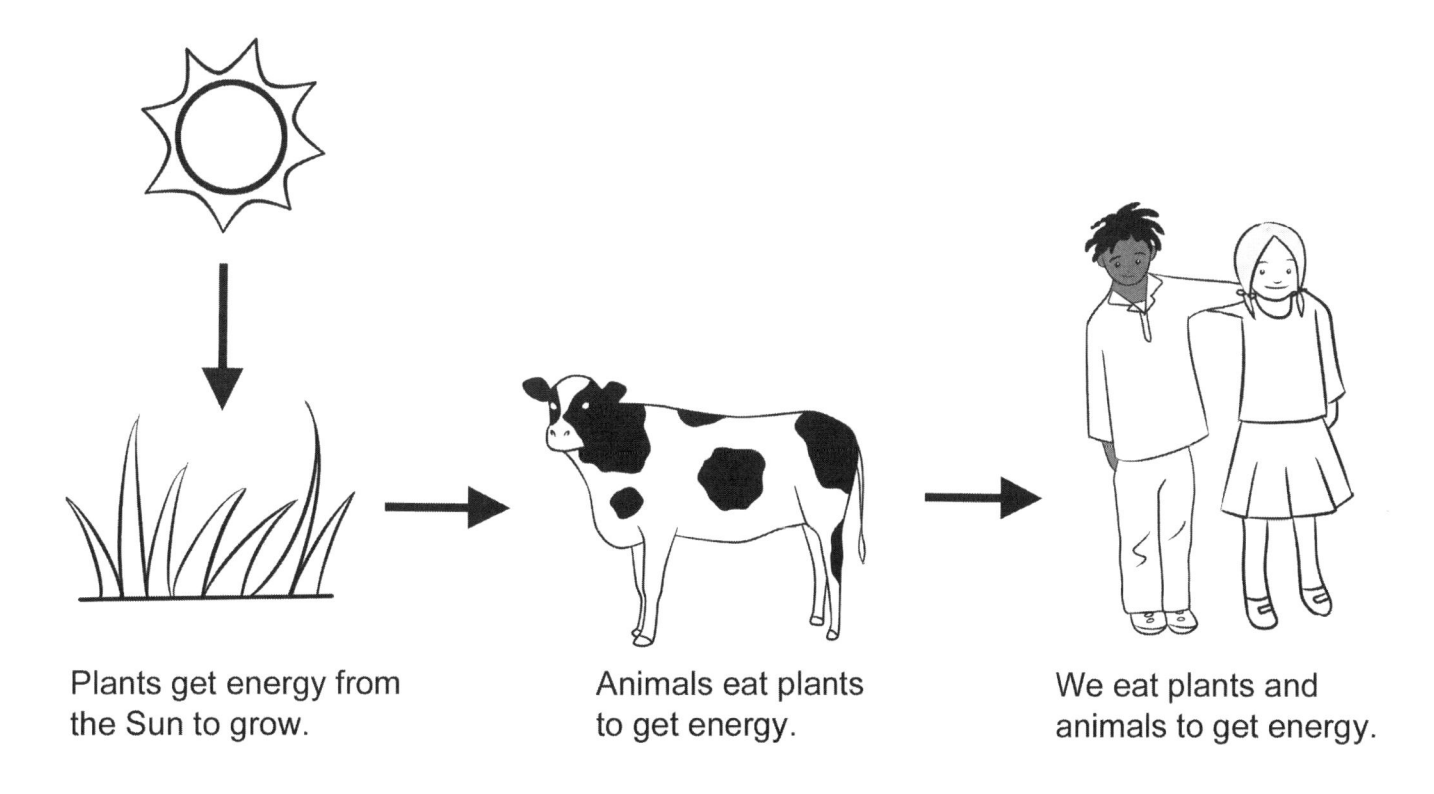

Plants get energy from the Sun to grow.

Animals eat plants to get energy.

We eat plants and animals to get energy.

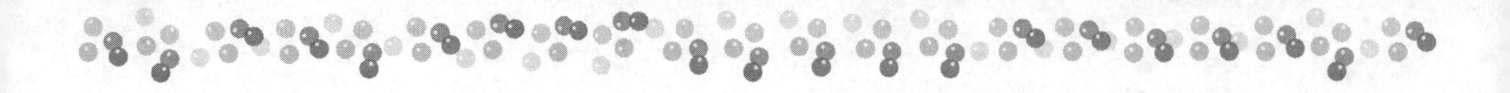

"We Get Energy from Food"—Think About It!

1. Label the diagram.

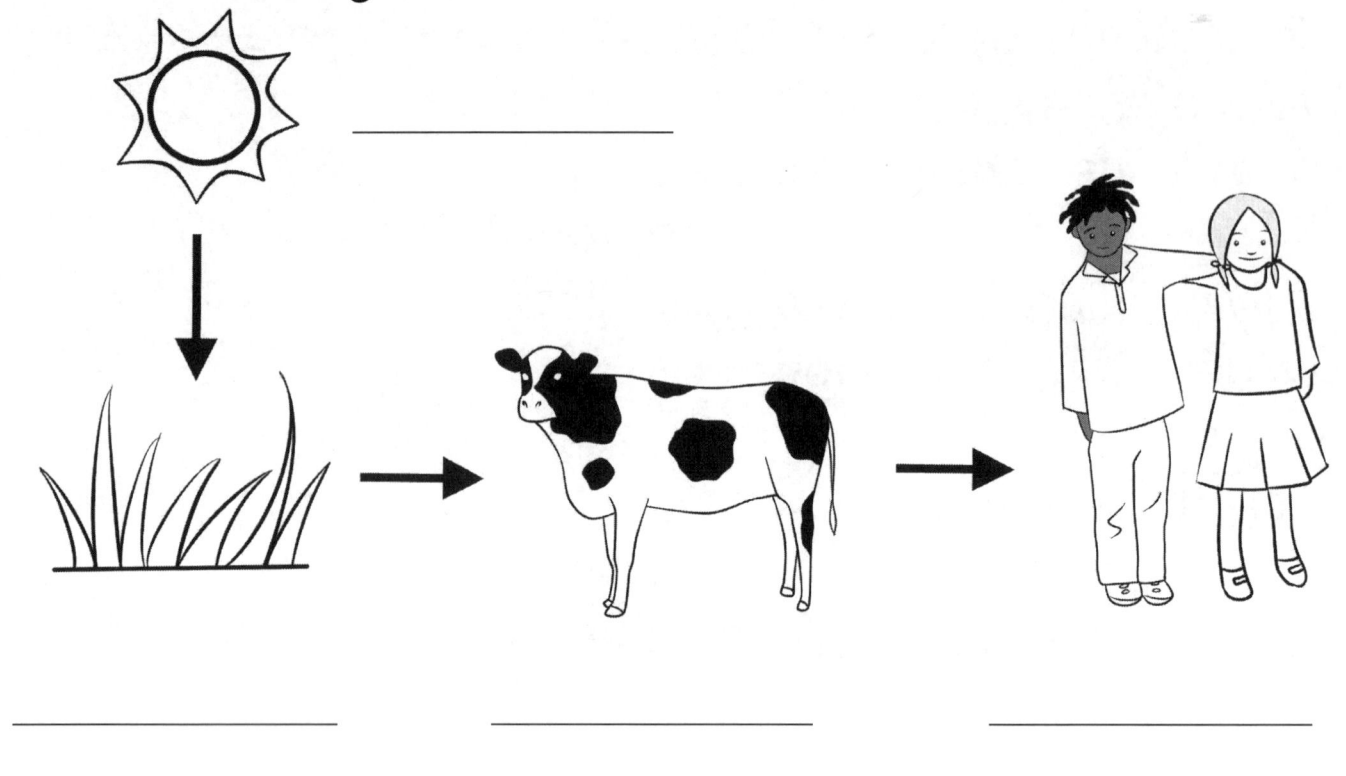

   _____

   _____   _____   _____

   _____   _____   _____

2. Complete each sentence. Use the words below.

   energy   animals   plants   Sun

   a) Plants get energy from the _____.

   b) Some animals eat plants to get _____.

   c) People eat _____ and _____

   to get energy.

Farmers

Farmers grow food. They plant seeds and care for plants. They pick fruits and vegetables.

Farmer picking apples

Farmers take care of animals. Chickens give eggs and meat. Cows give milk and meat.

Farmer taking care of her cows

Truck drivers take the food to stores.

Truck driver carrying vegetables

Store clerks sell the food.

Clerk selling food

© Chalkboard Publishing

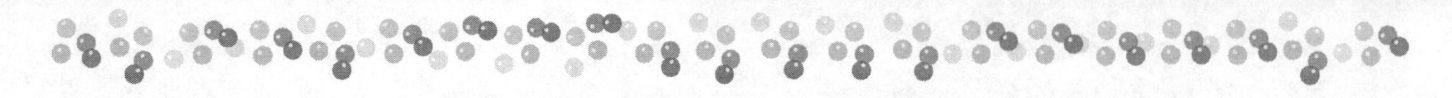

"Farmers"—Think About It!

1. What do farmers grow?

_____

2. Where does meat come from?

_____

3. Who takes the food to the stores?

_____

4. Who sells you food?

_____

5. Draw a picture of your family cooking food together. Show what you are cooking.

```
┌─────────────────────────────────────────────┐
│                                             │
│                                             │
│                                             │
│                                             │
│                                             │
│                                             │
│                                             │
└─────────────────────────────────────────────┘
```

Write a sentence about your picture.

_____

Energy at Work

Read how energy makes things work.

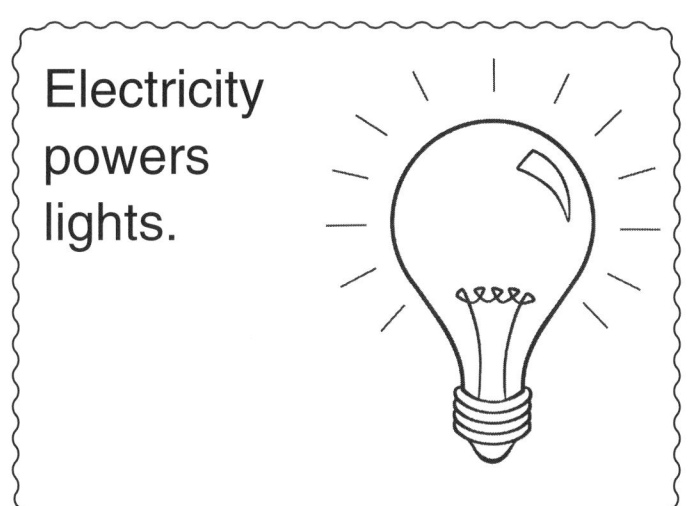

Electricity powers lights.

Wood, oil, and gas heat our homes.

Gasoline makes cars and buses move.

Batteries power flashlights and other things.

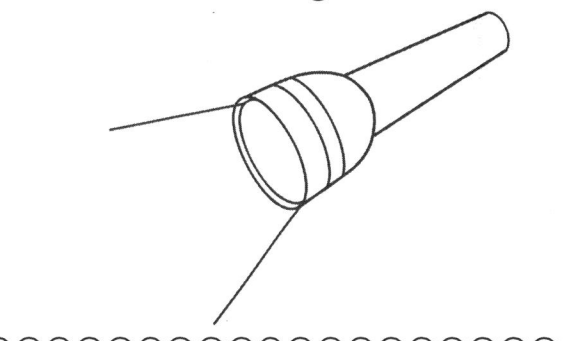

Brain Stretch

battery

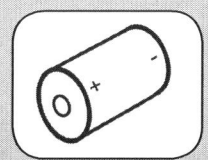

List two different things that need batteries to work.

"Energy at Work"—Think About It!

1. Write the source of energy for each item. Use the words below.

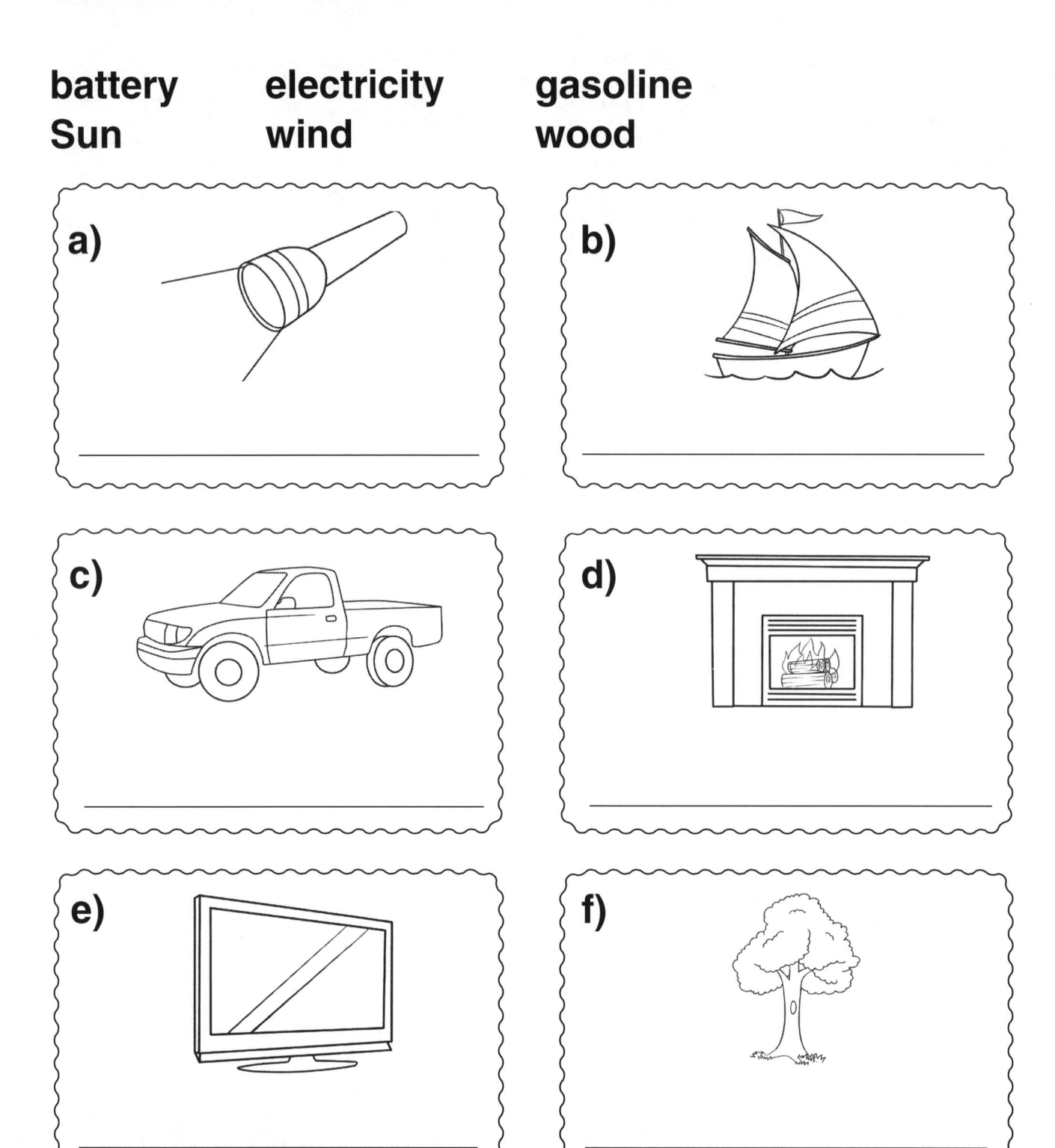

battery   electricity   gasoline
Sun   wind   wood

a) _____

b) _____

c) _____

d) _____

e) _____

f) _____

Activity: Energy Matching Game

1. Draw a line to match the source of energy with where the energy is used. Write what type of energy the source creates. Use the words below.

heat   light   movement   sound

a) wood   kite _____

b) wall outlet   campfire _____

c) battery   lamp _____

d) wind   radio _____

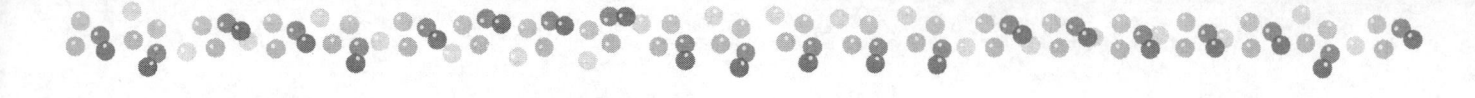

Activity: Build a Kite

A kite flies using energy from wind. Work with a partner to build a kite.

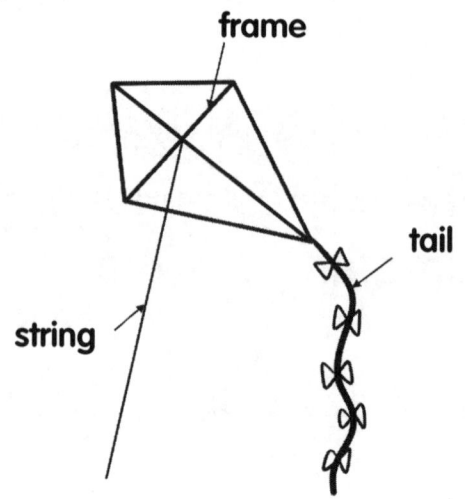

What You Need

- 2 wooden dowels (1 long, 1 short)
- Brown paper bag
- Duct tape
- String on a spool
- Scissors
- Stickers and markers or crayons

What You Do

1. Use string to tie the rods together to form a cross.

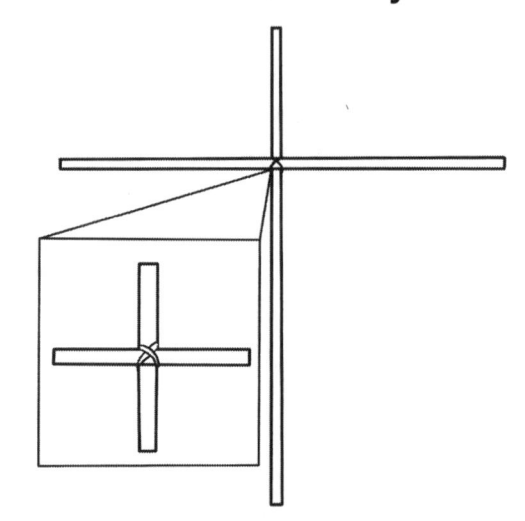

2. Put the cross frame on the brown paper.

3. Draw a kite shape on the paper. Draw the shape about 3 cm larger than the cross on all sides.

4. Cut out the shape. The shape should look like a diamond.

5. Fold down the extra paper on each diagonal.

6. Use tape to keep the folded paper in place. The tape will make four thick edges.

7. Tape the paper to the cross frame.

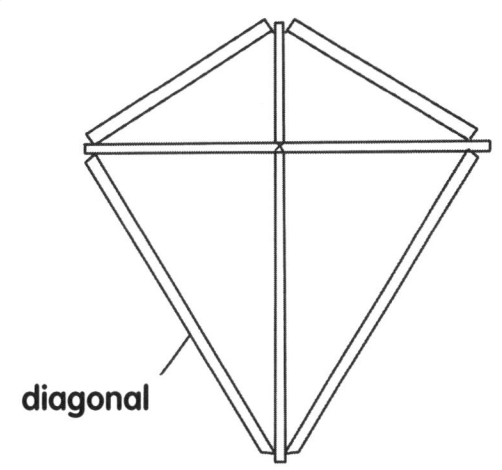

diagonal

8. Tie a long piece of string to the point where the rods cross. Leave the end of the string on the spool.

9. Draw on, colour, and put stickers on your kite.

10. Test your kite on a windy day.

Brain Stretch

Solve this riddle.

I am a type of balloon.
I have a large basket to carry people.
I need wind to move.
What am I?

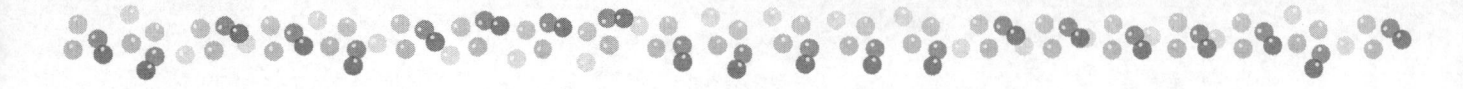

Wheels Go Round and Round

Wheels help things move. What has wheels?

A **bus** has wheels.

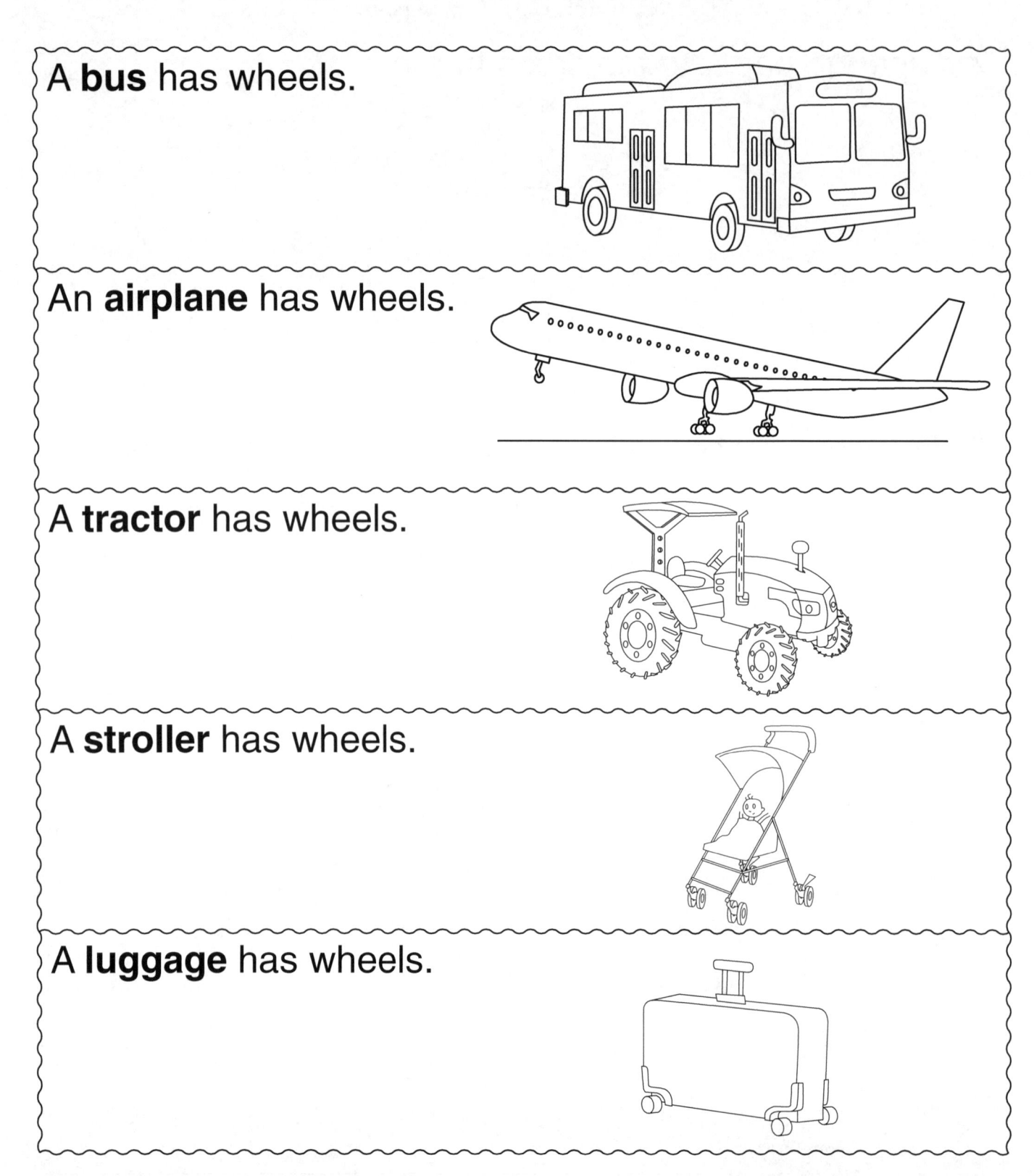

An **airplane** has wheels.

A **tractor** has wheels.

A **stroller** has wheels.

A **luggage** has wheels.

"Wheels Go Round and Round"—Think About It!

Answer each riddle. Use the words below.

bus   tractor   luggage   stroller   airplane

1. You fly in the sky in me. _____

2. You put clothes in me. _____

3. You find me at a farm. _____

4. A child rides in me. _____

5. Lots of people ride in me. _____

Draw something else that has wheels.

Activity: Energy From Foods

Make a healthy food collage.
Cut out pictures from magazines and paste them below.

Using Energy to Stay Warm and Cool

How to Stay Warm	How to Stay Cool
• Wear a sweater. • Turn on the heat. • Open the curtains to let in the sunlight.	• Stay in the shade or turn on a fan. • Go to cooled places. • Close the curtains to block the sunlight.

Think About It!

1. Draw a picture that shows how you do the following.

I stay warm in winter.

I stay cool in summer.

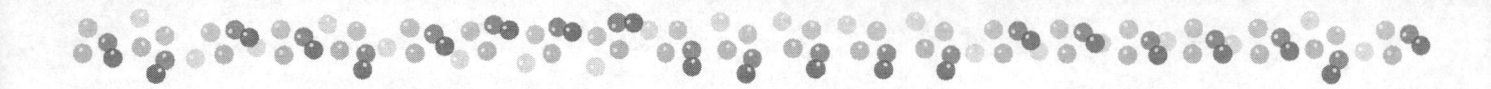

Saving Energy

Here are some ways to save energy.

- Turn off lights and electronics when you leave a room.

- Do not hold the refrigerator door open.

- Hang clothes on a line instead of using a dryer.

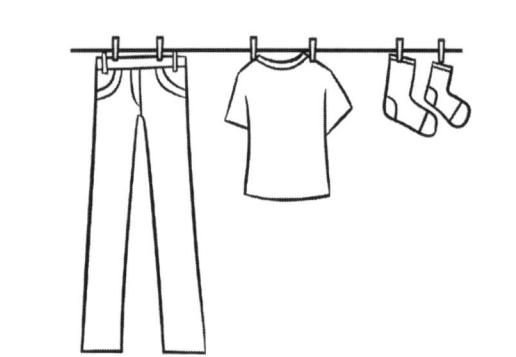

- Walk to school or ride a bike instead of taking a ride.

Create a poster of tips for how to save energy. Use a separate piece of paper.

"Saving Energy"—Think About It!

1. Write **S** if the action saves energy.
Write **W** if the action wastes energy.

   a) Turn off the television when no one is watching. _____

   b) Turn on the dishwasher only when it is full. _____

   c) Use the washer to clean only your pyjamas. _____

   d) Open the curtains on a hot day. _____

   e) Hold the refrigerator door open until you decide what to eat. _____

2. Draw something that uses a lot of energy in your home. Label the item. Write a sentence about how you could use this item less.

What Would You Do?

1. What would happen if you did not have electricity?

I would cook food on a camp stove.

a) What could you play instead of a video game? Draw a picture.

b) What could you use for light instead of a lamp? Draw a picture.

50

© Chalkboard Publishing

What I Learned About Energy

1. Fill in the blanks. Use the words below.

   electricity   energy   save   Sun

   a) The energy chain starts with the _____.

   b) People get _____ from food.

   c) My computer needs _____ to work.

   d) Turning off the light helps _____ energy.

2. Draw three things in your home that use energy. Write the source of energy each item uses.

3. Write one thing you can do to save energy.

   _____

Objects Are Made from Materials

Objects are things we use.
Objects are made from one or more materials.

fabric

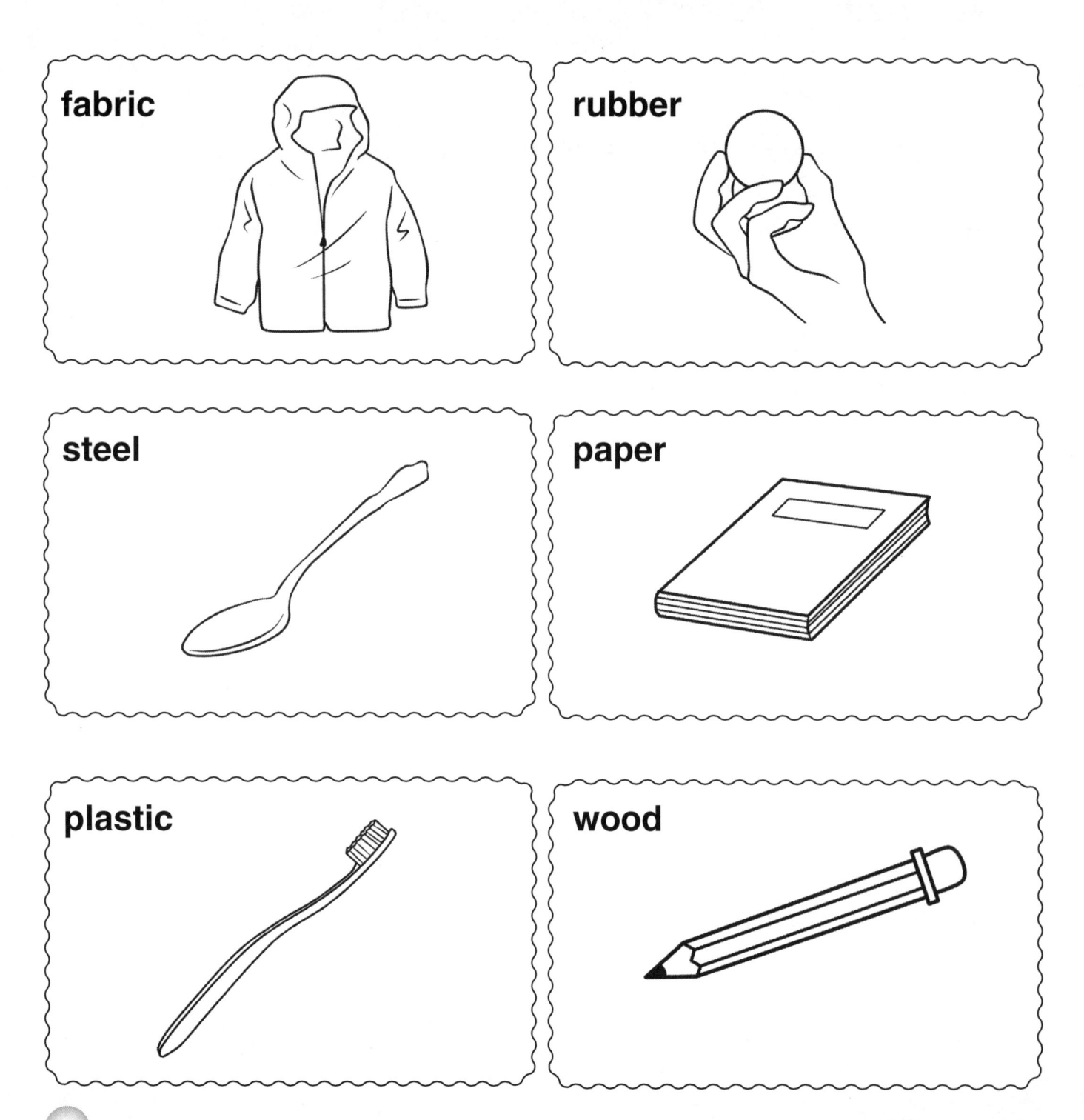

rubber

steel

paper

plastic

wood

"Objects Are Made from Materials"—Think About It!

1. Look in magazines for pictures of objects.
Find objects made from the materials below.
Cut out and paste one object for each material.

a) fabric

b) paper

c) plastic

d) rubber

e) steel

f) wood

2. Write a sentence about materials.

_____

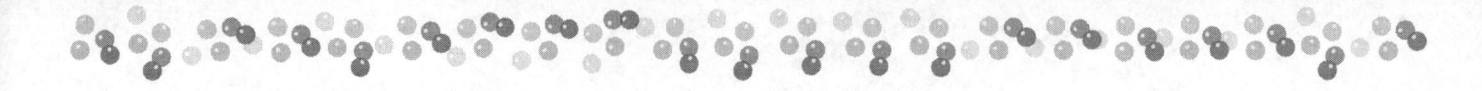

Activity: Find Objects

Objects are made from at least one material. Find objects in the classroom.

1. Draw and label an object that is made from each material.

a) fabric

b) plastic

c) steel

d) wood

Structures Are Made from Materials

A structure is the support frame of an object. Structures are made from different materials.

The tent is made from fabric called nylon.
The poles are metal.
The poles support the tent.
The poles are a structure.

A frame structure is like a skeleton. You can see through it.

Think About It!

1. Circle the structure below that was made by people. Draw a box around the structure found in nature.

web

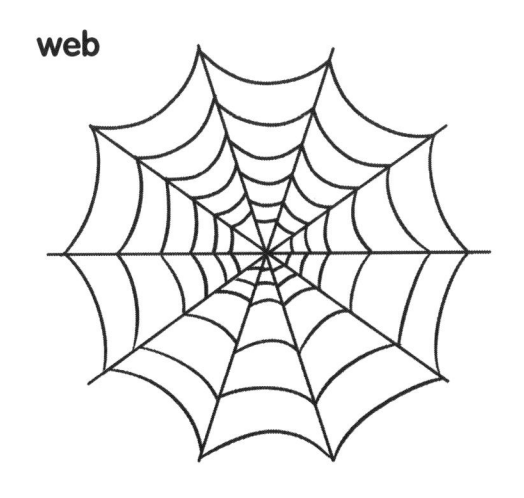

bridge

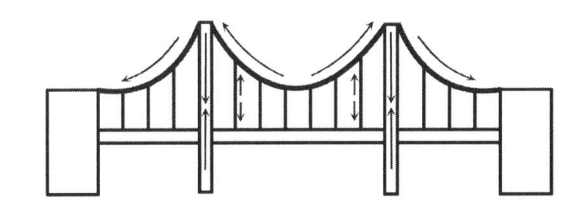

"Structures Are Made from Materials"—Think About It! (continued)

2. Is a bike a structure?   Yes   No

How do you know?

_____

3. Draw each structure.
List the materials that are used in the structure.

a) This structure is in a park. You can slide down it.

```
┌─────────────────────────────────────┐
│                                     │
│                                     │
│                                     │
│                                     │
└─────────────────────────────────────┘
```

_____

b) This structure opens up. You use it to stay dry in the rain.

```
┌─────────────────────────────────────┐
│                                     │
│                                     │
│                                     │
│                                     │
└─────────────────────────────────────┘
```

Natural and Manufactured Materials

Some materials are found in nature.

Rubber is made from the sap of rubber trees.

Wood comes from trees.
Some trees are made into boards.
Other trees are used for paper.

Materials Made by People

Materials such as fabric are made by people. These are called manufactured materials.

A beach pail is made from plastic.

Paper is made from tiny wood chips mixed with water.

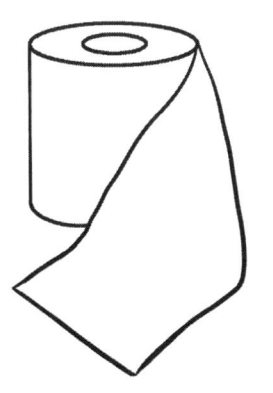

"Natural and Manufactured Materials"—Think About It!

1. Sort the words below into the right groups.
   Print the words.

   fabric   wool   plastic   tree sap   steel   wood

Natural Materials	Materials Made by People
_____	_____
_____	_____
_____	_____

Did You Know?

Some metals are natural.
These metals are found in rocks.
Metals such as steel are made by people.
Think of two other objects made from steel.

$1 coin

_____   _____

Where Do Materials Come From?

All materials made by people are made from natural things.
Paper is made from wood.
Rubber is made from tree sap.
Plastic is made from oil.
Steel is made from metals and minerals in rocks.
Fabric is made from natural materials.

Cotton comes from cotton plants.

Wool comes from sheep.

Think About It!

1. Draw a line from the material to what it is made from.

wool

paper

rubber

steel

fabric

tree sap

cotton

rock

tree

sheep

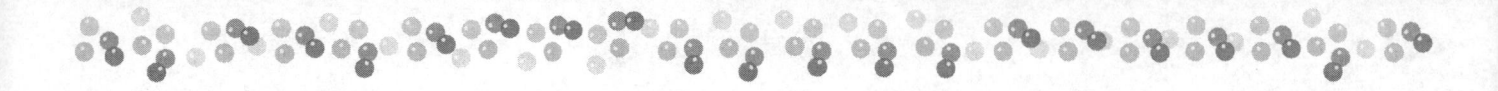

Activity: Describe Objects

Choose an object. Use your senses to describe it. Tell your partner about the object.

Object	What does it look like?	What does it feel like?	What is it made from?

The clock is made from plastic that feels hard and smooth. The clock wakes me in the morning.

The bag is made from plastic that is thin and flexible. This makes the bag easy to use and to store.

Did You Know?

There are many types of plastic. Some plastics are rigid. This means the plastic is hard to bend. Some plastics are flexible. This means the plastic is easy to bend.

"Activity: Describe Objects"—Think About It!

1. Cut out the word cards. Work with a partner. Read the descriptions on the cards below. Look for an object in the classroom to match each description. Write the name of the object. Tell what the object is made from.

smooth	**rough**
_____	_____
_____	_____

shiny	**dull**
_____	_____
_____	_____

rigid	**flexible**
_____	_____
_____	_____

soft	**hard**
_____	_____
_____	_____

More About Objects and Materials

It is important to choose the right materials to make an object. This helps an object do its job.

Sandpaper is made from paper with sand on it.
Sandpaper is rough and bumpy.
Sandpaper can be used to smooth off the rough edges on wood.

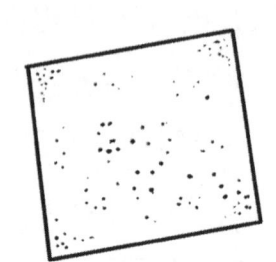

Scissors are made from plastic and steel.
The steel is sharp to be able to cut paper.
The plastic handles make the scissors easier to hold.

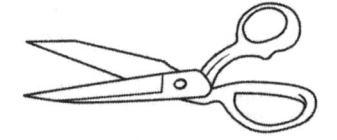

Think About It!

1. Footwear has different purposes.
   Name one material used to make each type of footwear.
   Explain your thinking to a partner.

   rubber boots

   skates

   slippers

Activity: Chairs Made from Different Materials

Chair seats can be made from different materials.

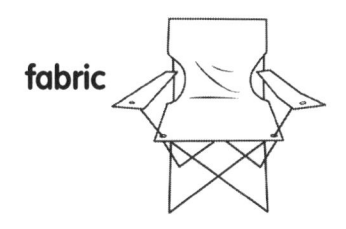

wood   plastic   fabric

1. Tell what you know about each type of chair. The first one is done for you.

What Materials the Chair Is Made From	What the Materials Are Made From	What I Know About the Materials
a) Wood	trees	• lasts a long time • strong • comfortable
b) Plastic seat and metal legs		
c) Fabric seat and metal legs		

© Chalkboard Publishing

Fasteners

Fasteners are objects that hold things together. There are many types of fasteners.

Zippers hold clothing together.

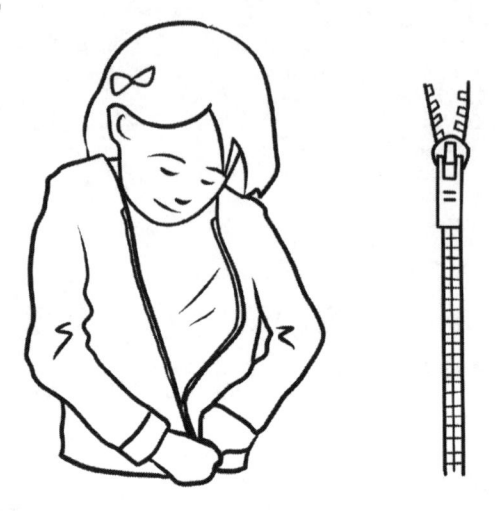

Tape and glue hold pieces of paper together.

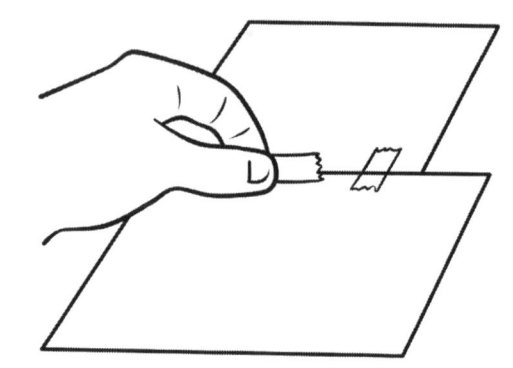

Nails join pieces of wood.

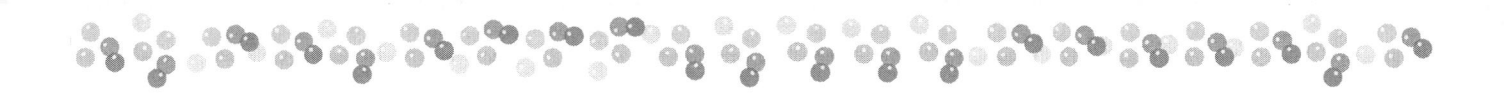

"Fasteners"—Think About It!

1. Draw the ways each fastener might be used.

a) glue

b) staples

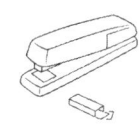

c) thread

d) button

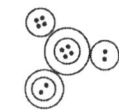

e) screw

f) push pin

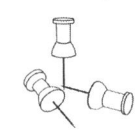

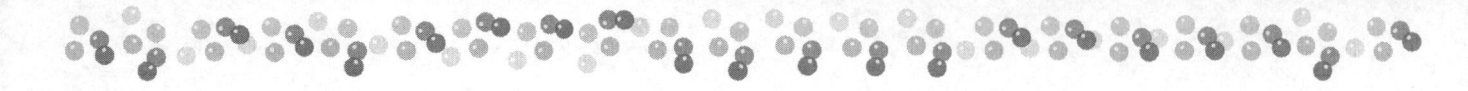

Tools for Cutting

We use **tools** to cut things. Tools that cut are **sharp**.

Scissors cut paper.

A **knife** cuts food.

A **saw** cuts wood.

A **lawnmower** cuts grass.

"Tools for Cutting"—Think About It!

What is the best tool to cut each object?
Fill in the blanks. Use the words below.

       scissors   **knife**   **saw**

1. Use a _____ to cut a board.

2. Use _____ to cut string.

3. Use a _____ to cut a cake.

4. Use _____ to cut ribbon.

Be safe! Sharp tools can cut you!

Experiment: Repelling Water

Water runs off or does not soak into some materials. This means the material the object is made from repels water.

Test to find out which materials repel water.

What You Need

- Plastic wrap, rubber balloon, cotton fabric, newspaper, and aluminum foil
- Paper towel, cut into 5 small pieces
- 5 foil pie plates
- 5 mL measure
- Water

What You Do

1. Predict which materials you think will repel water.
2. Record your predictions.
3. Put a small piece of paper towel in each foil pie plate.
4. Put one material over top of each piece of paper towel. Make sure the paper towel does not stick out!
5. Ask an adult to pour 5 to 10 mL of water on each material. Wait for 2 minutes.
6. Ask an adult to remove the material from each pie plate without spilling the water.
7. Check the paper towel pieces.
8. Record your results.

"Experiment: Repelling Water"—Think About It!

1. Record your predictions. Then record the results.

Material	My Prediction: Will it repel water?		My Results: Does it repel water?	
	YES	NO	YES	NO
Plastic wrap				
Rubber balloon				
Cotton fabric				
Newspaper				
Aluminum foil				

2. What do the results tell you?

_____

3. Rubber boots keep your feet dry. What makes the boots waterproof?

_____

_____

rubber boots

Experiment: Absorbing Water

Water soaks into some materials.
This means the material the object is made from absorbs water.

Test to find out which materials absorb water.

What You Need

- Plastic wrap, soft sponge, Styrofoam food tray, newspaper, and cotton fabric
- 5 foil pie plates
- 5 mL measure
- Water

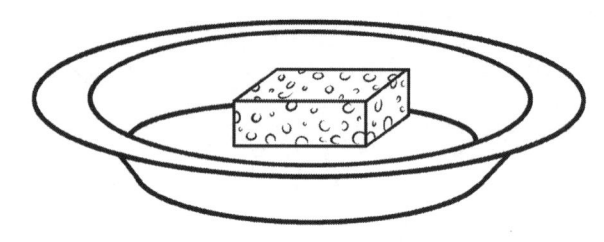

What You Do

1. Predict which materials you think will absorb water.

2. Record your predictions.

3. Place the materials in the pie plates, one type per plate.

4. Ask an adult to put 5 to 10 mL of water on top of each material. Wait for 2 minutes.

5. Check the materials.

6. Record your results.

"Experiment: Absorbing Water"—Think About It!

1. Record your predictions. Then record the results.

Material	My Prediction: Will it absorb water?		My Results: Does it absorb water?	
	YES	NO	YES	NO
Plastic wrap				
Soft sponge				
Styrofoam food tray				
Newspaper				
Cotton fabric				

2. What do the results tell you?

_____

3. Circle the object that you think absorbs water best.

wood   paper towels   steel pan

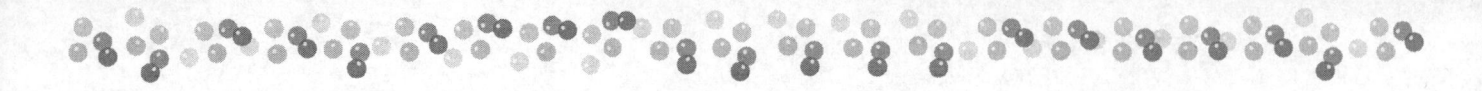

Activity: How to Reduce Waste

What can we do with objects when they are no longer useful?
What can we do with an old chair?

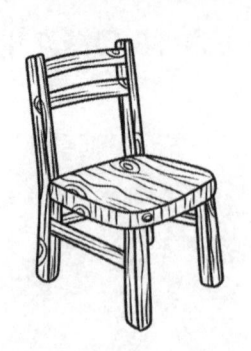

- We could reuse the wood to make a small table.
- We could give the chair away.
- We could use the chair for a different purpose.

1. The old chair materials can be reused. Draw a different way to use them.

2. Write a sentence about how you can use the new object.

Activity: Build a Structure

Build a structure. Use recycled materials.

Here are some ideas:

- Bird feeder
- Tent for a pet
- Musical instrument

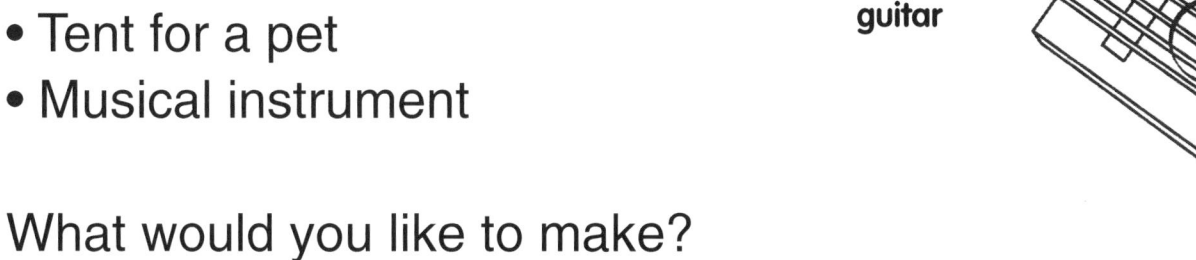

guitar

What would you like to make?

_____

Draw the structure below.

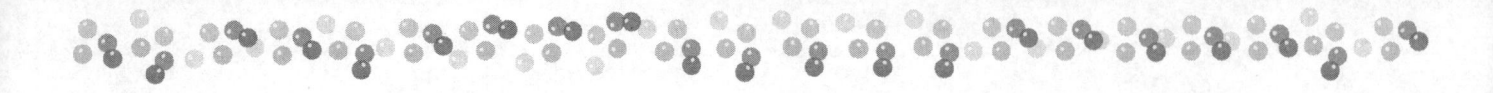

"Activity: Build a Structure"—Think About It!

1. What is the purpose of your structure?

_____

2. List the materials.
   Tell why you chose the materials you used.

Material	Why I Used This Material

3. What did you use to hold the structure together?

_____

4. In what ways can you use your structure?

_____

What I Learned About Materials and Structures

1. Fill in the blanks. Use the words below.

   fastener   flexible   material   nature   structure

   a) Wood is a _____.

   b) A bridge is a _____.

   c) Materials are made by people or found in _____.

   d) Plastic can be rigid or _____.

   e) A button is a type of _____.

2. An object must be made from the right materials to do its job well. Draw an object made from each material below.

a) plastic	b) steel	c) wood

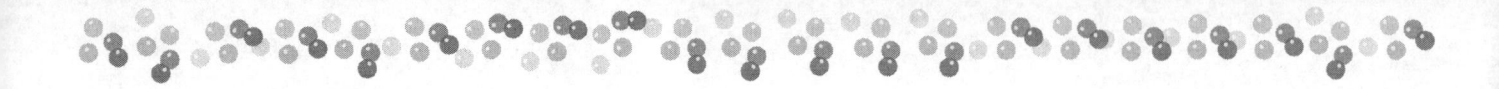

Day and Night

Each day, the Sun rises and sets.
This is called the day and night cycle.
A cycle is a pattern that repeats.

Draw pictures of activities for each of the following times.

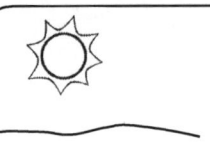

The Sun rises in the morning.
When the Sun is in the sky, it is **day**.

The Sun sets at the end of the day.
When there is no Sun in the sky, it is **night**.

Types of Cycles

1. Circle the cycles you know about.

      days of the week   **months of the year**   **seasons**

2. Cut out the pictures about a child's daily cycle. Put the pictures in the order they happen.

Light and Heat Change What We Do

The Sun is our main source of light and heat. Sometimes, what we do depends on sunlight and heat. On sunny days, the air is usually warmer.

swim

hike

play

On most nights, there is very little light and less heat.

sleep

watch the stars

watch fireworks

What Is It Like Outside?

There are different types of weather.
Temperature tells you how warm or cold it is outside.

1. Match the item you might use with each type of weather.

The weather is sunny.

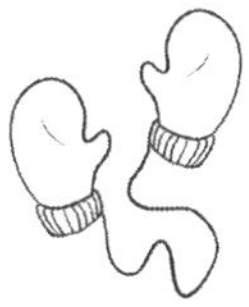

The weather is rainy.

The weather is snowy.

The weather is windy.

The weather is cool.

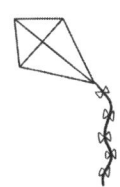

Brain Stretch

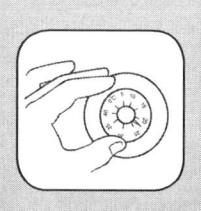

Circle the item that is used in hot weather.
Draw a square around the item that is used in cold weather.

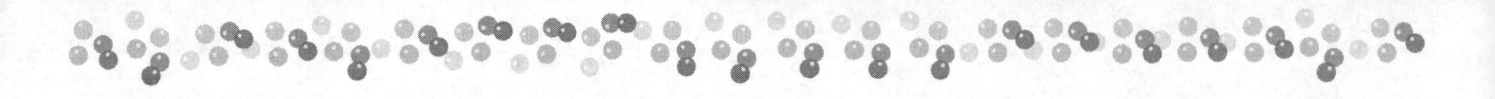

"What Is It Like Outside?"—Think About It!

2. What will it be like outside when you wear these types of clothing? Use the words below.

hot   warm   cool   cold

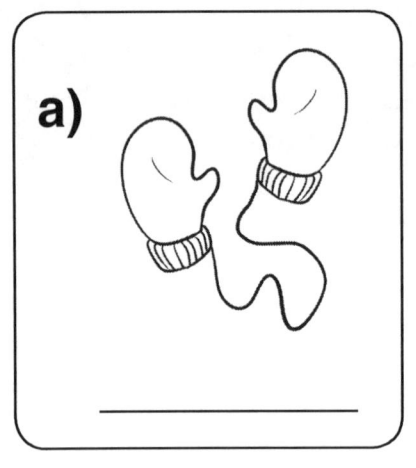

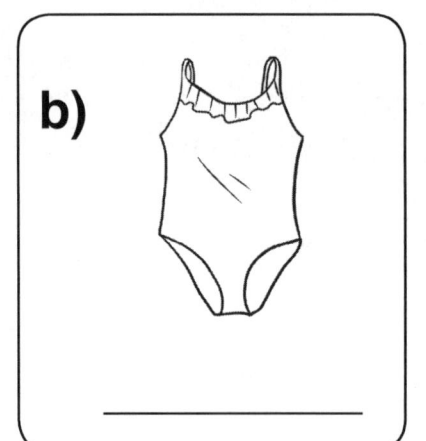

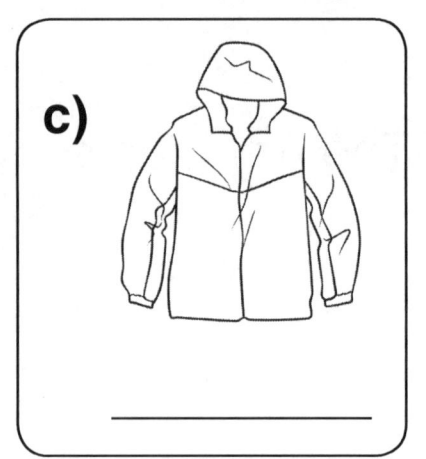

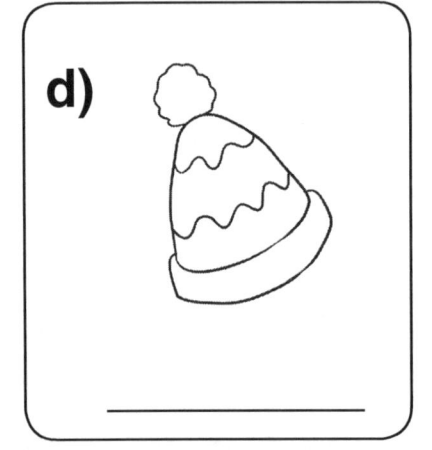

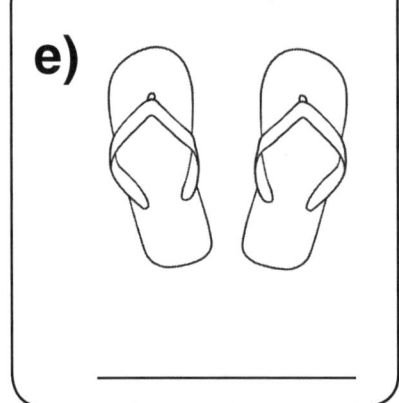

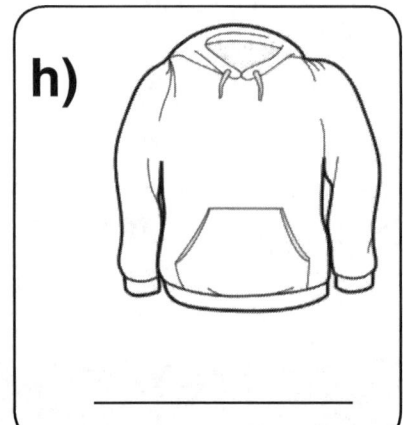

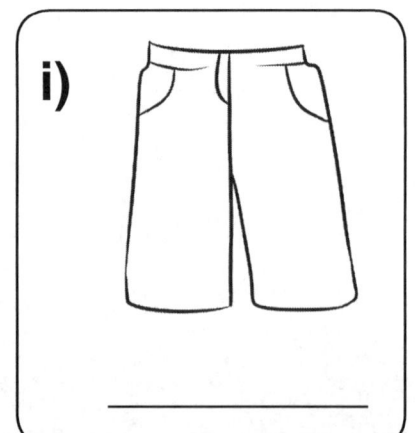

a) _____

b) _____

c) _____

d) _____

e) _____

f) _____

g) _____

h) _____

i) _____

Experiment: Compare Temperatures

Find out whether the temperature changes during the day.

What You Need

- Thermometer

What You Do

1. Measure the outdoor temperature at school. Measure the temperature in the morning, at noon, and at the end of the day. Do this for five days.
2. Use the words below to fill in the blanks. A word can be used more than once.

cooler   warmer

I predict that the temperature will be...

_____ in the morning

_____ at noon

_____ in the afternoon

© Chalkboard Publishing

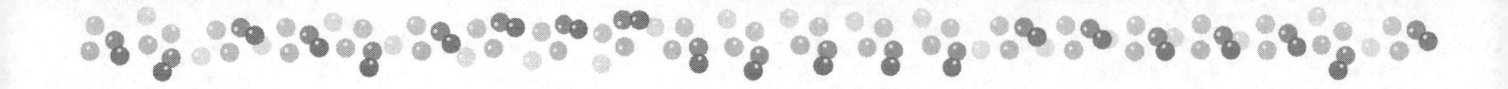

"Experiment: Compare Temperatures"—Think About It!

1. With the help of an adult, record the results.

Day	Morning	Noon	Afternoon
1			
2			
3			
4			
5			

2. Does the temperature change during the day? **Yes   No**

3. Fill in the blanks. Use the words below.

afternoon   morning   noon

a) The temperature is the warmest at _____.

b) The temperature is cooler in the _____ and the _____.

The Four Seasons

In many places, the weather changes during the year.
In many places, the seasons change, too.
Draw a picture for each season.

Spring

In spring, the snow melts.
It gets warmer and rains.
Flowers and plants start
to grow.
The days are longer.
The nights are shorter.

Summer

In summer, it gets hot.
Flowers are in bloom.
The days are long.
The nights are short.

continued next page

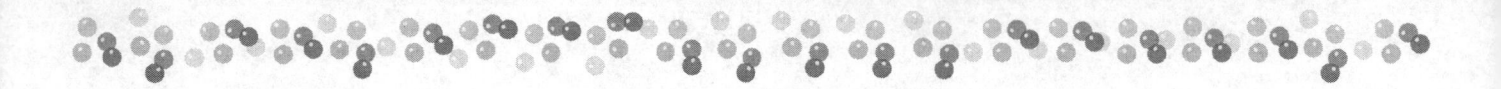

Draw a picture for each season.

Fall

In fall, it gets cooler.
Some trees shed leaves.
The days are shorter.
The nights are longer.

Winter

In winter, it is cold.
Many plants die.
There is snow and ice.
The days are short.
The nights are long.

"The Four Seasons"—Think About It!

1. Are the seasons a cycle?   **Yes**   **No**

How do you know? _____

2. Label the pictures. Use the words below.

fall   **winter**   **spring**   **summer**
cool   **long days**   **short days**   **warm**

a) _____

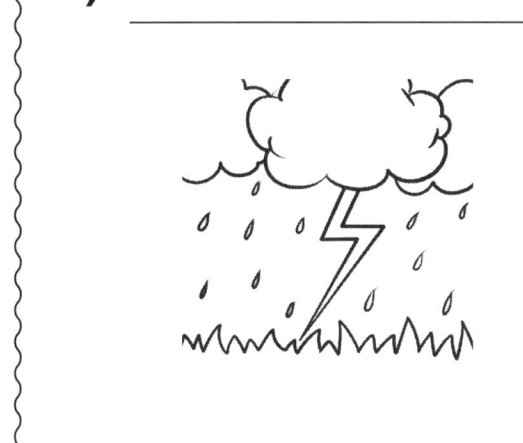

b) _____

c) _____

d) _____

The Seasons Make Plants Change

Plants change as the seasons change.

Spring
- Trees start to bud.
- Plants and seeds begin to grow.
- Grass turns green.
- Spring flowers bloom.

Summer
- Trees have lots of leaves.
- Flowers grow and bloom.
- Grass grows.
- Some plants have seeds.

Fall
- Leaves change colour.
- Leaves fall off the trees.
- Fruit can be picked off some types of trees.

Winter
- The trees have no leaves.
- Plants stop growing.
- Some plants die.

"The Seasons Make Plants Change"—Think About It!

1. Label the pictures of apple trees. Use the words below.

spring   summer   fall   winter

a) The apple tree has ripe apples.

_____

b) The apple tree has lots of leaves.

_____

c) The apple tree has lost its leaves.

_____

d) The apple tree is in bloom.

_____

The Seasons Make Animals Change

Animals change as the seasons change.

Spring
- Many animals are born or hatch.
- Parent animals feed and raise their babies.

Summer
- Many insects appear.
- Animals need to stay cool. Some sleep in the shade. Bats hang in cool, dark caves. Birds splash in water to cool down.

Fall
- Some birds migrate, or fly south, to where the weather is warmer. Butterflies migrate, too.
- Some animals collect food for the winter.

Winter
- Animals such as bears hibernate, or go to sleep.
- Animals such as dogs grow thick fur to keep warm.
- Some animals change colour. Some rabbits grow a white coat to hide in the snow.

"The Seasons Make Animals Change"—Think About It!

1. Draw a line to match the animal with what the animal does. Write the name of the season in which this happens.

a) Dog

Feed their babies

Season: _____

b) Butterfly

Hibernates

Season: _____

c) Parent animals

Migrates

Season: _____

d) Bear

Keeps cool in the shade

Season: _____

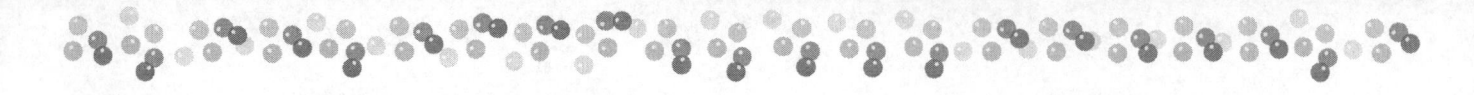

The Seasons Change What We Do

Some outdoor activities can only be done in certain seasons.

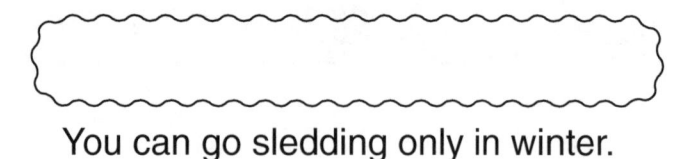

You can go sledding only in winter.

Some outdoor activities can be done in any season.

~~You can skate and play hockey in an arena.~~ Arenas can create ice in all seasons.

~~You can swim at a community~~ centre in all seasons.

Farmers can grow food in winter. ~~They use a greenhouse to grow~~ plants in cold weather.

"The Seasons Change What We Do"—Think About It!

1. Write the season in which each activity can be done. Use each word once.

spring   summer   fall   winter

a) _____

b) _____

c) _____

d) _____

2. Circle the activity that can be done in only one season.

3. How could one activity be done in a different season?

_____

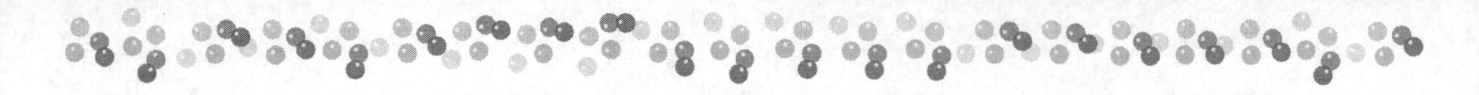

Activity: What Do You Wear?

Draw something you like to do outside in each season. Show what you wear. Circle your favourite season.

Spring	**Summer**
Fall	**Winter**

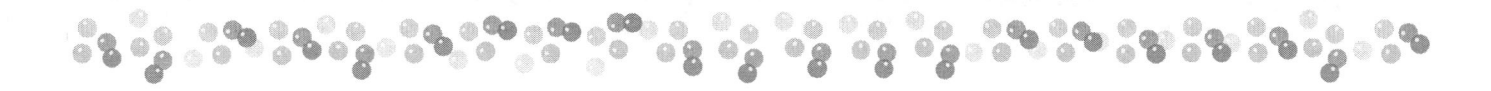

The Seasons and the Environment

How we use energy depends on the season.

The weather gets colder in fall. We turn on the heat in our homes to keep warm.

In summer, the air is hot. We turn on the air conditioner to keep cool. We fill the outdoor pool with water. Then we can swim to cool off.

All these things use energy. Energy is used to power the furnace. Energy is used to pump water and heat the pool.

We need to be careful about the energy we use.
Here are some ways to use less energy.

In the winter, turn down the heat. Put on a sweater.

On a hot day, close the curtains to block the sunlight.

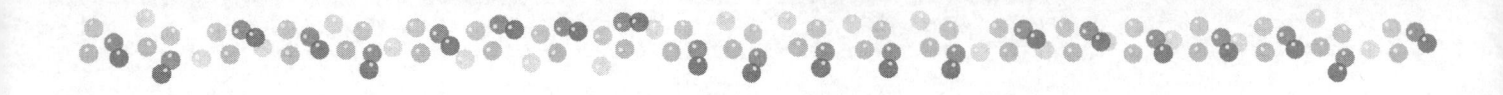

"The Seasons and the Environment"—Think About It!

1. Complete each sentence. Use the words below.

cool   energy   furnace   heat

a) Energy is used to _____ a pool.

b) Energy is used to heat a home with a _____.

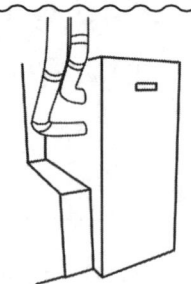

c) _____ is used to create ice in summer.

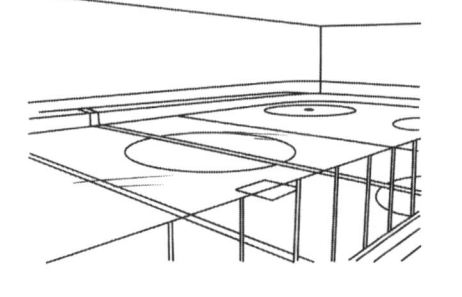

d) Energy is used to _____ a home with an air conditioner.

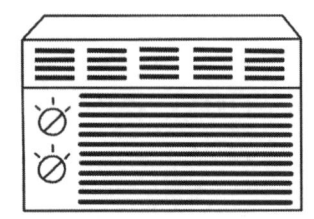

Did You Know?

In summer, we use a lot of water. We water the garden and the grass. We play with the water hose. Using a lot of water reduces our supply of water.

What I Learned About the Seasons

1. Fill in the blanks. Use the words below.

   cooler   cycle   summer   warmer   winter

   a) A pattern that repeats is a _____.

   b) The longest days are in _____.

   c) The longest nights are in _____.

   d) The temperature is often _____ at noon than in the morning.

   e) The temperature is often _____ in the afternoon than it is at noon.

2. Use a separate piece of paper.

   a) Fold the paper in half.
   b) Then fold it in half again to make four squares.
   c) Use one square for each season.
   d) Print the name of the season at the top of the square.
   e) Draw one thing animals do during that season.
   f) Label each picture.

Engineering in Our Daily Lives

Engineers design and build things we use every day. Cut out and paste pictures of things that engineers designed. Some examples include a toothbrush, or a video game.

Think Like an Engineer!

An engineer is a person who designs and build things. Engineers want to understand how and why things work. Engineers try different ideas, learn from their mistakes, then try again. Engineers call these steps the design process.

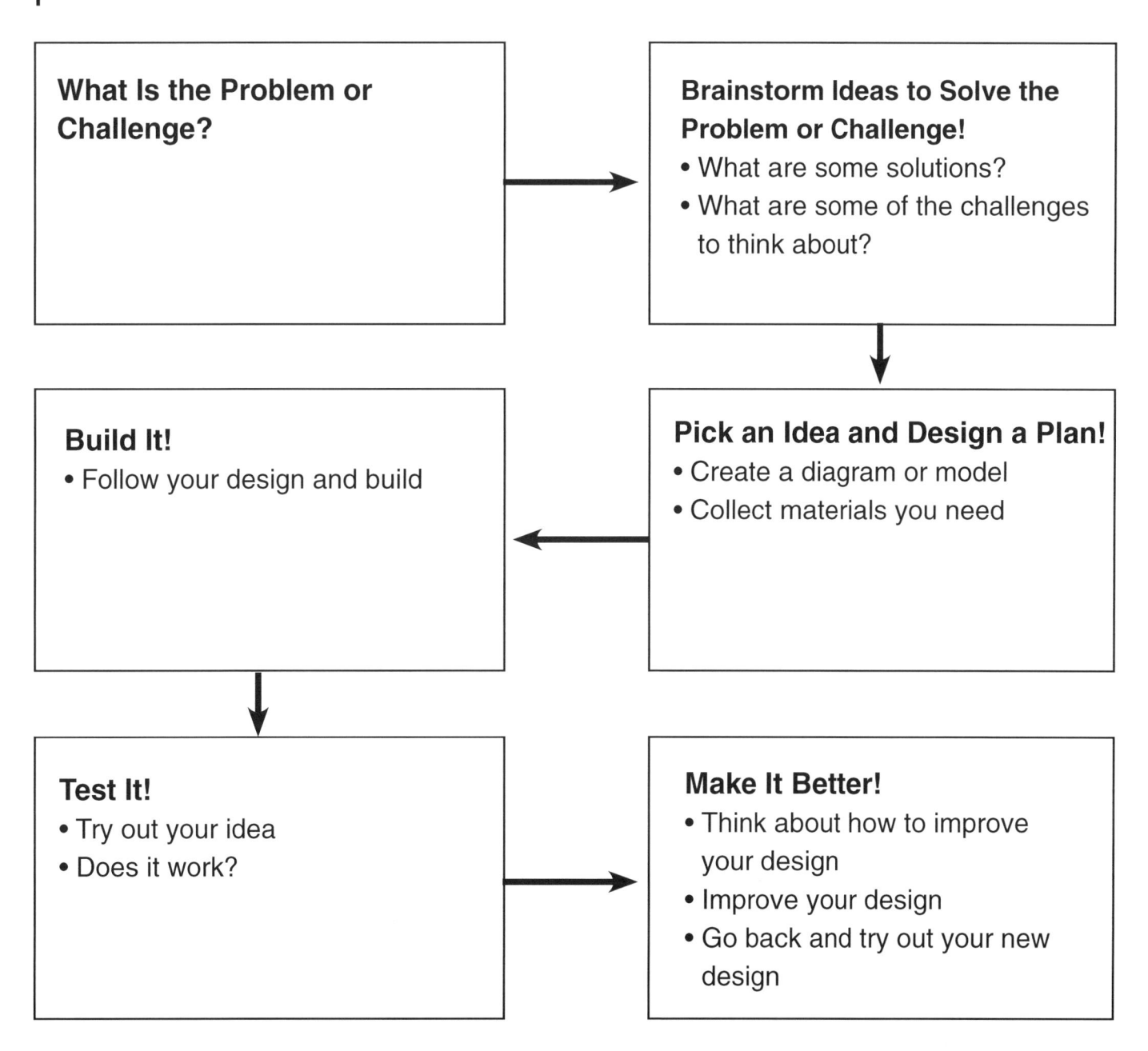

What Is the Problem or Challenge?

Brainstorm Ideas to Solve the Problem or Challenge!
- What are some solutions?
- What are some of the challenges to think about?

Pick an Idea and Design a Plan!
- Create a diagram or model
- Collect materials you need

Build It!
- Follow your design and build

Test It!
- Try out your idea
- Does it work?

Make It Better!
- Think about how to improve your design
- Improve your design
- Go back and try out your new design

Remember to be patient. Take your time to figure things out.

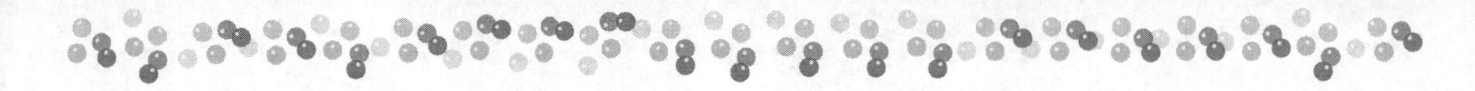

The Design Process

1. What is the problem or challenge?

_____

_____

2. Think about it! What are some ideas to solve the problem or challenge?

_____

_____

_____

_____

_____

_____

_____

continued next page

3. Pick a design idea! Draw and label a picture of your design. Write about your plan.

continued next page

4. Get ready! What materials do you need?

continued next page

5. Test it! Build your design and try it out.

Did it work?   Yes ☐   A little ☐   No ☐

6. Make it better! How can you make your design better?

_____

_____

7. Try your design out again. What happened?

_____

_____

8. What do you wonder about?

_____

_____

9. What are you proud of?

_____

_____

Engineering Challenges

1. Build a cardboard city using found materials.
2. Build a marble run using found materials or construction toys.
3. Build the tallest structure you can using paper cups and craft sticks.
4. Build a home for a pet.
5. Design an umbrella using materials such as straws, tape, plastic, cloth, and so on. Test the umbrella using a squirt bottle. See how well it repels water.

Materials to Keep On Hand

Measuring Tools

calculator	clock	measuring cup	measuring spoons
measuring tape	ruler	scale	timer

Materials

aluminum foil	balloons	balls	bubble wrap
buckets	cardboard	cardboard boxes	cloth
construction paper	corks	cotton swabs	elastics
flour	foam	foam cubes	glue
glue gun	glue sticks	magnets	modelling clay
paper clips	paper cups	paper fasteners	paper towel tubes
pipe cleaners	pipe sections and joints	plastic containers	rice
sand	sandpaper	scissors	stapler
straws	string	Styrofoam	Stryofoam cups
tape	tissue	tissue paper	toothpicks
twist ties	wood	wooden craft sticks	yarn

Promoting STEM Occupations

STEM Dramatic Play Centre

A dramatic play centre promotes students' practice of language skills through the communication of ideas and dramatic play. Set up a drama centre to represent a specific place of work so students can gain experiences in a variety of STEM-related occupations. Each time a new drama centre is created, be sure to discuss as a class the ways in which STEM skills for each of the jobs are important. Encourage families to contribute items that will help make the dramatic play centre more authentic. In addition, invite special guests who occupy STEM-related work roles to speak with students. Here are a few ideas.

Restaurant – provide a table, chairs, plastic place settings, plastic food, cookbooks, receipt paper, and play money. Have students create and design a class restaurant menu with price list. Roles for students may include chef, server, and cashier.

Veterinary Clinic – provide picture cards of animals, stuffed or plastic animals, patient information forms, medical tools and supplies, exam table, and X-rays. Roles for students may include veterinarian, pet owner, and veterinary technician or assistant.

Space Station – provide a space station control panel, headsets, spacesuits and helmets, astronaut ID badges, launch checklist, captain's log, an experiment to complete, chairs with seatbelts, pictures of the planets, and empty food tubes. Roles for students may include astronaut, engineer, mission specialist, and Mission Control Centre worker.

STEM Class Big Book

As a class, publish a big book. Assign one page of the class big book to each student or have students work in small cooperative groups. The complexity of the class big book will depend on students' abilities. For example, students can print a missing word to complete a sentence, and create an illustration for a page. Or students could create drafts first, then plan how to lay out their page. You may wish to allow students to take the big book home for a night to share with their families. Each page can explain how different devices make people's lives easier, or pages can describe different STEM occupations.

STEM Occupation Riddle Cards

Help students develop their knowledge of STEM occupations using riddle cards as prompts. Activate prior knowledge by providing students with occupation details and requesting the occupation name for an answer. Use these cards as a springboard for discussion. Create more riddle cards as a class.

STEM-Related Occupations

To learn more about some of these occupations visit the following websites:

http://www.sciencebuddies.org/science-engineering-careers

https://kids.usa.gov/watch-videos/index.shtml

Accountant
Aerospace Engineer
Agricultural Engineer
Agricultural Technician
Aircraft Mechanic and Service Technician
Animal Breeder
Animal Trainer
Animator
Anthropologist
Architect
Astronaut
Astronomer
Athletic Trainer
Audio Engineer
Audiologist
Automotive Mechanic
Biochemical Engineer
Biochemist/Biophysicist
Biologist
Biology Teacher
Biomedical Engineer
Business Owner
Cardiovascular Technician
Carpenter
Chef
Chemical Engineer
Chemical Technician
Chemistry Teacher
Chiropractor
Civil Engineer
Civil Engineering Technician
Climate Change Analyst
Clinical Psychologist
Computer Engineer
Computer Programmer
Computer Systems Analyst
Construction Manager
Counselling Psychologist
Dietetic Technician

Dietitian and Nutritionist
Doctor
Electrical Engineering Technician
Electrician
Electronics Engineer
Emergency Medical Technician
Environmental Engineer
Environmental Engineering Technician
Environmental Restoration Planner
Environmental Scientist
Epidemiologist
Fire-Prevention Engineer
Fish and Game Worker
Food Science Technician
Food Scientist and Technologist
Forest and Conservation Technician
Forest and Conservation Worker
Geoscientist
Graphic Designer
Hydrologist
Industrial Engineer
Interior Designer
Landscape Architect
Manufacturing Engineer
Marine Architect
Marine Biologist
Math Teacher
Mechanical Engineer
Mechanical Engineering Technician
Medical Lab Technician
Medical Scientist
Meteorologist
Microbiologist
Microsystems Engineer
Mining and Geological Engineer
Molecular and Cellular Biologist
Neurologist
Nuclear Engineer
Nursery and Greenhouse Manager
Nutritionist

Occupational Health and Safety Specialist
Optical Engineer
Optometrist
Paleontologist
Patent Lawyer
Pathologist
Park Ranger
Petroleum Engineer
Pharmacist
Physical Therapist
Physician
Physician Assistant
Physicist
Pilot
Psychologist
Registered Nurse
Respiratory Therapist
Robotics Engineer
Robotics Technician
School Psychologist
Seismologist
Software Developer (Applications)
Software Developer (Systems Software)
Soil and Plant Scientist
Soil and Water Conservationist
Space Scientist
Speech-Language Pathologist
Statistician
Transportation Engineer
Transportation Planner
Urban Planner
Veterinarian
Video Game Designer
Volcanologist
Water/Wastewater Engineer
Wind Energy Engineer
X-ray Technician
Zookeeper
Zoologist
Wildlife Biologist

When I Grow Up...

I would like to be a _____

because _____

_____.

STEM Occupation Riddle Cards

STEM Occupation Clues — 1

- I am a type of doctor who checks teeth and gums.
- I can fix problems with teeth.
- I check that teeth grow properly.
- I tell people how to take care of their teeth.

What am I?

Answer: A dentist

STEM Occupation Clues — 2

- I am someone who studies ancient people.
- I find and look at things that people left behind long ago.
- I want to understand how they lived, what they looked like, and their traditions.
- I am like a detective, and I use special tools to dig in dirt.
- I often work outdoors.

What am I?

Answer: An archaeologist

STEM Occupation Riddle Cards

STEM Occupation Clues　　　　　　　　　　**3**

- I am someone who works with wires that carry electricity.

- It is my job to make sure there is electricity in many places such as homes, factories, and other buildings.

- I can fix problems with wires or fuses, too.

- I sometimes work indoors and sometimes work outdoors.

What am I?

Answer: An electrician

STEM Occupation Clues　　　　　　　　　　**4**

- I am someone who takes care of wild animals.

- I give them food each day.

- I help train the animals, too.

- Sometimes I answer people's questions about the animals.

What am I?

Answer: A zookeeper

STEM Occupation Riddle Cards

STEM Occupation Clues — 5

- I am someone who designs buildings such as homes, skyscrapers, and malls.

- I draw a plan of how a building will look.

- I work with engineers, construction workers, and electricians to build structures to make sure the building is safe for people.

What am I?

Answer: An architect

STEM Occupation Clues — 6

- I am someone who works with pipes used to carry water, gas, or waste.

- I check pipes for leaks and make sure they are working.

- I will come to buildings or homes to fix broken pipes.

- I also fix sinks, tubs, and toilets.

- I sometimes work indoors, and sometimes work outdoors.

What am I?

Answer: A plumber

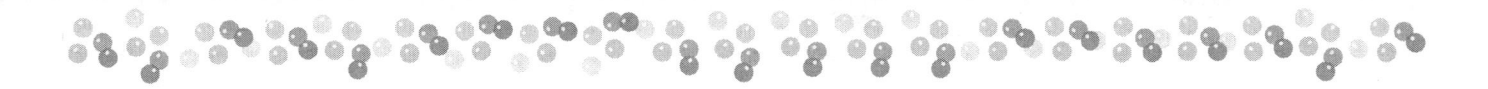

STEM Occupation Riddle Cards

STEM Occupation Clues — 7

- I am someone who studies weather patterns.

- I predict the weather for people to let them know if will be a rainy, cloudy, or snowy day.

- I use maps to explain the weather to people.

What am I?

Answer: A meteorologist

STEM Occupation Clues — 8

- I am someone trained to be a pilot or crew member on a spacecraft.

- Sometimes I do experiments while staying at a space station.

- Sometimes I need to fix equipment in outer space.

What am I?

Answer: An astronaut

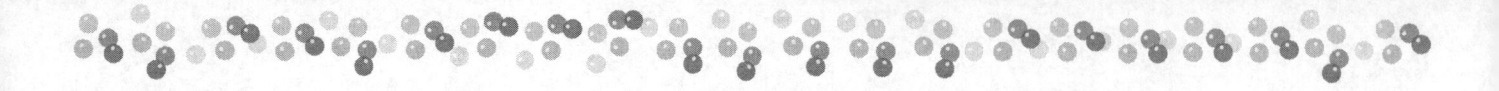

STEM Occupation Riddle Cards

STEM Occupation Clues — 9

- I am someone who wants to know how and why things work.

- I use science to plan out and build things.

- I plan out and build things to make people's lives easier.

- I sometimes work indoors, and sometimes work outdoors.

What am I?

Answer: An engineer

STEM Occupation Clues — 10

- I am someone who cooks food for people.

- I know how to mix ingredients to make food tasty.

- I am in charge of the kitchen in a restaurant.

What am I?

Answer: A chef

A Web Organizer About...

_____

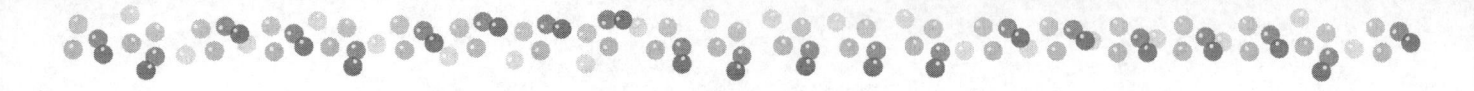

STEM Vocabulary

Keep a list of new STEM words you have learned. Make sure to include the definition for each word.

Word	Definition

How Am I Doing?

	Completing my work	**Using my time wisely**	**Following directions**	**Keeping organized**
Full speed ahead!	• My work is always complete and done with care. • I added extra details to my work.	• I always get my work done on time.	• I always follow directions.	• My materials are always neatly organized. • I am always prepared and ready to learn.
Keep going!	• My work is complete and done with care. • I added extra details to my work.	• I usually get my work done on time.	• I usually follow directions without reminders.	• I usually can find my materials. • I am usually prepared and ready to learn.
Slow down!	• My work is complete. • I need to check my work.	• I sometimes get my work done on time.	• I sometimes need reminders to follow directions.	• I sometimes need time to find my materials. • I am sometimes prepared and ready to learn.
Stop!	• My work is not complete. • I need to check my work.	• I rarely get my work done on time.	• I need reminders to follow directions.	• I need to organize my materials. • I am rarely prepared and ready to learn.

© Chalkboard Publishing

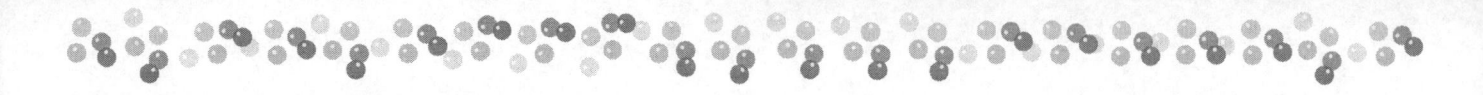

STEM Rubric

	Level 1 Below Expectations	Level 2 Approaches Expectations	Level 3 Meets Expectations	Level 4 Exceeds Expectations
Knowledge of STEM Concepts	• Displays little understanding of concepts. • Rarely gives complete explanations. • Intensive teacher support is needed.	• Displays a satisfactory understanding of most concepts. • Sometimes gives appropriate, but incomplete explanations. • Teacher support is sometimes needed.	• Displays a considerable understanding of most concepts. • Usually gives complete or nearly complete explanations. • Infrequent teacher support is needed.	• Displays a thorough understanding of all or almost all concepts. • Consistently gives appropriate and complete explanations independently. • No teacher support is needed.
Application of STEM Concepts	• Relates STEM concepts to outside world with extensive teacher prompts. • Application of concepts rarely appropriate and accurate.	• Relates STEM concepts to outside world with some teacher prompts. • Application of concepts sometimes appropriate and accurate.	• Relates STEM concepts to outside world with few teacher prompts. • Application of concepts usually appropriate and accurate.	• Relates STEM concepts to outside world independently. • Application of concepts almost always appropriate and accurate.
Written Communication of Ideas	• Expresses ideas with limited critical thinking skills. • Few ideas are well organized and effective.	• Expresses ideas with some critical thinking skills. • Some ideas are well organized and effective.	• Expresses ideas with considerable critical thinking skills. • Most ideas are well organized and effective.	• Expresses ideas with in-depth critical thinking skills. • Ideas are well organized and effective.
Oral Communication of Ideas	• Rarely uses correct STEM terminology when discussing STEM concepts.	• Sometimes uses correct STEM terminology when discussing STEM concepts.	• Usually uses correct STEM terminology when discussing STEM concepts.	• Consistently uses correct STEM terminology when discussing STEM concepts.

Notes: _____

STEM Focus _____

Student's Name	Knowledge of STEM Concepts	Application of STEM Concepts	Written Communication of Ideas	Oral Communication Skills	Overall Mark

© Chalkboard Publishing

STEM Expert!

You are doing great!

Great Work!

Keep up the effort!

ANSWER KEY

Unit: Needs of Living Things

Living Things, pages 2–3
1. All living things need food, water, and air.
2. Yes, because the squirrel grows, moves, and needs food, water, and air to live.
3. Students should circle the man, dog, cow, and flower.

Living Things Collage, page 4
Sentences will vary, but should show an understanding that all living things grow, move, and need food, water, and air.

Non-living Things Collage, page 5
Sentences will vary, but should show an understanding that all non-living things do not grow, move, or need food, water, or air.

My Body, page 6

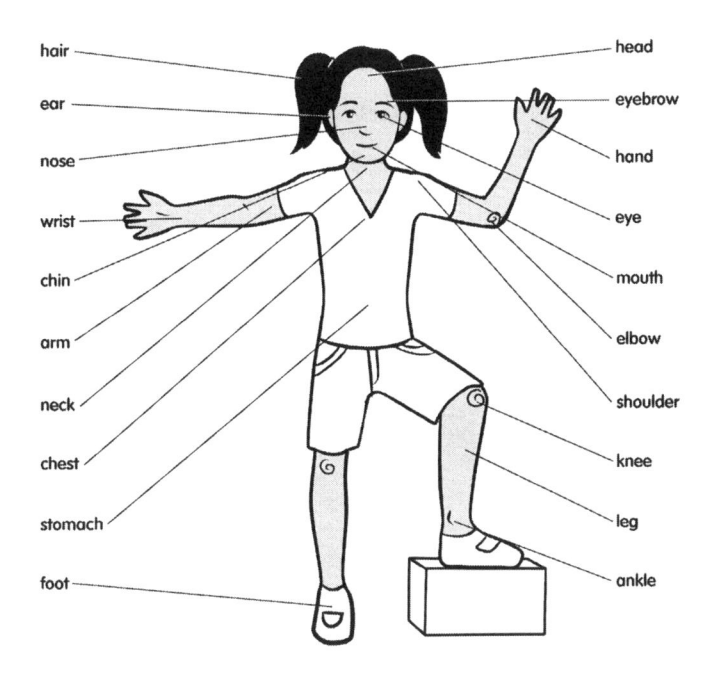

Labels: hair, ear, nose, wrist, chin, arm, neck, chest, stomach, foot, head, eyebrow, hand, eye, mouth, elbow, shoulder, knee, leg, ankle

Your Body Helps You, pages 7–8
1. muscles
2. teeth
3. brain
4. fingers
5. lungs
6. heart
7. bones

Your Five Senses, pages 9–11
1. eyes
2. ears
3. fingers
4. nose
5. tongue
6. a) smell; b) touch; c) hearing; d) taste; e) sight

Listen for Sounds, pages 12–13
1. car
2. start
3. fire
4. cross

Animals On the Move, page 14
1. a) rabbit; b) turtle; c) tiger; d) monkey

Compare Living Things, page 15
Answers will vary, depending on what two living things the student chooses to compare.

Parts of a Plant, pages 16–17
1. a) flower; b) stem; c) leaves; d) roots
2. Sample answers: Same—both have leaves; both are plants. Different—one has a flower, the other does not; one is tall and the other is short.

Experiment: How Do Plants Take Up Water? pages 18–19
1. Students should notice red dots, indicating that the food colouring is being drawn into the stalk. On the second day, the whole stalk and the leaves should be tinted red.
2. The stem helps the plant take up water.

Brain Stretch, page 20
Sample answer: A chipmunk gets air, food, water, and shelter from its environment.

Animals Live in Different Places, page 21
1. a) moose—forest; b) duck—pond; c) whale—ocean; d) owl—tree; e) bee—hive

A Healthy Environment, page 22
You might wish to create a bulletin board display of students' drawings.

People Can Harm Living Things, pages 23–24
1. Sample answer: Polluted water might make the fish sick or kill them.
2. Check that students' drawings show a way to help the environment.
3. Check that students' sentences tell something about their drawing.

Taking Care of Living Things, page 25
Answers will vary.

What I Learned About Living Things, page 26
1. a) plants; b) air, water; c) stem; d) environment
2. a) nose; b) eyes; c) ears

© Chalkboard Publishing

ANSWER KEY

Unit: Energy

Brain Stretch, page 27
Students should say that food gives them the energy they need to grow.

What Is Energy? pages 27–28
1. jump
2. energy
3. create
4. Students should circle B, C, D, and F.

Where Energy Comes From, page 29
1. Answers will vary.
2. You may wish to ask students to share their answers with the class.

We Get Energy from the Sun, page 30
1. Drawings will vary, but should show what the Sun's light and heat do.

Experiment: What Does Sunlight Do to Water? pages 31–32
1. Answers may vary. Students may predict that the water in the sunlight will get warmer.
2. Answers may vary.
3. Answers may vary, but should indicate that the water in the sunlight has a higher temperature than the water in the shade.
4. a) warm; b) cool

Experiment: What Does Sunlight Do to Plants? pages 33–34
1. Answers may vary.
2. Drawings should show that the plant in the sunlight is still healthy and green, whereas the plant in the dark is spindly, yellow, and almost dead.
3. Sample answer: The plant that did not get sunlight turned yellow, weak, and nearly died.
4. sunlight

We Get Energy from Food, pages 35–36
1. Labels, counterclockwise from the top: Sun, plants, animals, humans
2. a) Sun; b) energy; c) animals, plants

Farmers, pages 37–38
1. Farmers grow fruits and vegetables.
2. Meat comes from cows and chickens.
3. Truck drivers take the food to the stores.
4. Store clerks sell us the food.
5. Ensure that students' drawings show their family cooking food together. Ensure that students write a sentence about their picture.

Brain Stretch, page 39
Sample answers: toys, flashlight, radio, portable music player, cell phone, camera.

Energy at Work, pages 39–40
1. a) battery; b) wind; c) gasoline; d) wood; e) electricity; f) the Sun

Activity: Energy Matching Game, page 41
1. a) Wood—campfire, heat; b) Electrical outlet—lamp, light; c) Battery—radio, sound; d) Wind—kite, movement

Activity: Build a Kite, page 42
You might wish to organize a kite-flying day in the schoolyard, or ask students to come up and show their kites to the class.

Brain Stretch, page 43
I am a hot-air balloon.

Wheels Go Round and Round, pages 44–45
1. airplane
2. luggage
3. tractor
4. stroller
5. bus

Activity: Energy from Foods, page 46
You might wish to create a bulletin board display of students' healthy food collages.

Using Energy to Stay Warm and Cool, page 47
1. Answers will vary, but should correctly reflect the seasons.

Saving Energy, pages 48–49
1. Students should write **S** for (a) and (b), and **W** for (c), (d), and (e).
2. Answers will vary.

What Would You Do? page 50
1. Sample answers: a) play a board game or card game, b) use a candle or flashlight

What I Learned About Energy, page 51
1. a) Sun; b) energy; c) electricity; d) save
2. Answers will vary.
3. Answers will vary.

Unit: Materials, Objects, and Structures

Objects Are Made from Materials, pages 52–53
1. Check that students have correctly identified the materials the objects are made from. You may wish to ask students to share their choices with the class.
2. Answers will vary.

Activity: Find Objects, page 54
1. Check that students have correctly identified the materials the objects are made from. You may wish to ask students to share with the class.

© Chalkboard Publishing

ANSWER KEY

Structures Are Made from Materials, pages 55–56
1. Students should draw a circle around the bridge and a box around the spider web.
2. Yes. Because it is a support frame and you can see through it.
3. a) Slide: metal and plastic; b) Umbrella: metal, and plastic or fabric

Natural and Manufactured Materials, pages 57–58
1. Natural Materials: wool, tree sap, wood
   Materials Made by People: fabric, plastic, steel

Did You Know? page 58
Sample answers: spoon, car, hammer, bicycle frame, legs on a desk, door handle

Where Do Materials Come From? page 59
1. rubber—tree sap; fabric—cotton; steel—rock; paper—tree; wool—sheep

Activity: Describe Objects, pages 60–61
Ask students to share their choices with the class. Check that the object matches the description.

More About Objects and Materials, page 62
Sample answers: Boots—rubber; Skates—leather, metal, and fabric; Slippers—rubber and fabric

Activity: Chairs Made from Different Materials, page 63
1. Sample answers:
   b) Plastic chair: plastic is made from oil, and steel is made from metals and minerals taken from rocks; strong at the beginning, plastic becomes rough and cracked through years of use, metals can break and rust
   c) Fabric chair: fabric is made from cotton or vinyl, and steel is made from metals and minerals taken from rocks; not very strong, fabric can rip or break and does not last long, metals can break and rust

Fasteners, pages 64–65
1. Sample answers:
   a) Glue: join paper together
   b) Staples: join two or more pieces of paper
   c) Thread: join fabric together
   d) Button: join two parts of a piece of clothing together
   e) Screw: join two pieces of wood together
   f) Push pin: join a piece of paper together with a cork bulletin board

Tools for Cutting, pages 66–67
1. saw
2. scissors
3. knife
4. scissors

Extension: Discuss with students safety issues related to things that are sharp. For example, you might discuss topics such as the following:
- Cutlery knives are not sharp, so are safe for children to use. Other types of knives are very sharp and children should not touch them.
- Children can play with a toy saw because it is not sharp. Children should never touch or try to use a real saw.
- Children should avoid touching other kinds of objects that are sharp, such as broken glass or razor blades.

Experiment: Repelling Water, pages 68–69
1. Results should show that the plastic wrap, rubber balloon, and aluminum foil repel water.
2. Answers may vary.
3. The boots are made from rubber, which repels water and is therefore waterproof.

Experiment: Absorbing Water, pages 70–71
1. Results should show that the soft sponge, newspaper, and cotton fabric absorb water.
2. Answers may vary.
3. Students should circle the paper towels.

Activity: How to Reduce Waste, page 72
You might wish to ask students to share their ideas for different ways to use old chair materials.

Activity: Build a Structure, pages 73–74
You might wish to ask a few students to share their drawings and answers with the class.

What I Learned About Materials and Structures, page 75
1. a) material; b) structure; c) nature; d) flexible; e) fastener
2. Sample answers: a) reusable food container; b) hammer; c) bird house

Unit: Daily and Seasonal Changes

Day and Night, page 76
Pictures should clearly show the difference between what they do in the morning and what they do at night.

Types of Cycles, page 77
1. Answers will vary.
2. Child gets out of bed when the sun is shining; eats cereal for breakfast; does work at school; eats lunch; reads a story with family members; then sleeps.

Light and Heat Change What We Do, page 78
Discuss the pictures with students and ask what other activities they do in warm weather and at night.

Brain Stretch, page 79
Students should circle the fan and draw a square around the thermostat.

What Is It Like Outside? pages 79–80
1. Sunny—sunglasses; Rainy—umbrella; Snowy—mittens; Windy—kite; Cool—jacket
2. a) cold; b) hot; c) cool; d) cold; e) hot; f) warm; g) cold; h) cool; i) warm

© Chalkboard Publishing

ANSWER KEY

Experiment: Compare Temperatures, pages 81–82
1. Answers will vary. Make sure students are reading the thermometer correctly.
2. yes
3. a) noon; b) morning, afternoon

The Four Seasons, pages 83–85
1. Yes. Sample answer: Every year, the seasons get hotter from spring to summer, cooler from summer to fall, colder from fall to winter, and warmer from winter to spring.
2. a) spring, warmer; b) summer, longest days; c) fall, cooler; d) winter, shortest days

The Seasons Make Plants Change, pages 86–87
1. a) fall; b) summer; c) winter; d) spring

The Seasons Make Animals Change, pages 88–89
1. a) Dog: keeps cool in the shade; summer
   b) Butterfly: migrates; fall
   c) Parent animals: feed baby animals; spring
   d) Bear: hibernates; winter

The Seasons Change What We Do, pages 90–91
1. a) winter; b) spring; c) fall; d) summer
2. Students should circle (a) building the snowman, which can only be done in winter.
3. Sample answer: Swimming can be done indoors in winter.

Activity: What Do You Wear? page 92
Sample answers:
Spring: Sweater or hoodie, light jacket, pants, running shoes; riding a bicycle
Summer: T-shirt, shorts, flip-flops, bathing suit; swimming
Fall: Hoodie, light jacket, pants, running shoes; playing soccer
Winter: hat, mittens, warm coat, snow pants, boots; sledding

The Seasons and the Environment, pages 93–94
1. a) heat; b) furnace; c) energy; d) cool

What I Learned About the Seasons, page 95
1. a) cycle; b) summer; c) winter; d) warmer; e) cooler
2. Look for clear differences in what animals do during each season.

Engineering in Our Daily Lives, page 96
You might wish to create a bulletin board display of students' collages.